Shout S

A Portra

MW00942124

by J.H. Clark

Published in the United States by Lulu Press, Inc.

www.lulu.com

ISBN 978-1-7948-3540-5

Printed in the United States of America

DESIGN & COVER DESIGN BY J.H. CLARK

9 781794 835405

Dedicated to my husband and child
for their unending love and support.
Ron Clark
Kit Clark

In honor of the memory of my mentor,
Joel Williamson, Professor Emeritus,
University of North Carolina-Chapel Hill,
for his encouragement and understanding of history.

Democratizing Heaven

“The white parson, in his sermon to a colored congregation, seemed to hint that in heaven there must be some Jim Crow partition, with the white saints on one side and the black saints on the other. And after the sermon, when one of the black deacons was called on to pray, he got his chance to reply to this white preacher; for like many praying people, the old black man knew how to talk to the Lord and talk to other people, in the same phrases, and by attaching ‘riders’ to privileged prayers. He therefore prayed as follows:

‘And, O Lord, we thank thee fer the brother preacher who has spoke to us,—we thank thee for heaven,—we thank thee that we kin all go to heaven,—but as to that partition, O Lord, we thank thee that we’se a shoutin’ people,—we thank thee that we kin shout so hard in heaven that we will break down that partition an’ spread all over heaven,—an’ we thank thee that if the white folks can’t stand it, they can git on out of heaven an’ go to elsewhere!’”[1]

"For the history of the American Negro is unique also in this: that the question of his humanity, and of his rights therefore as a human being, became a burning one for several generations of Americans, so burning a question that it ultimately became one of those used to divide the nation."

— James Baldwin, "Stranger in the Village",
Notes of a Native Son[2]

Introduction

Shout So Hard to Heaven: A Portrait of Robert Charles

This book is based on actual events that took place in New Orleans leading up to and during Monday, July 23 through Friday, July 27, 1900. Historian and professor William Ivy Hair thoroughly researched this event and presented it in his 1976 book, *Carnival of Fury: Robert Charles and the New Orleans Race Riot of 1900*[3], from which the events portrayed in this book have been taken.

Most of the characters in *Shout So Hard to Heaven* are real, particularly Robert Charles, Henry Charles, Lenard Pierce, Virginia Banks, Lewis Forstall, Fred Clark, the Jacksons, the Nixons, Major Hearsey, the New Orleans police officers, Judge Chrisman, and all other individuals central to the narrative. However, much of their dialogue as well as a few outlying characters are based on my extensive study and understanding of the social environment, political atmosphere, and cultural life of the times, especially race relations.

In researching this narrative nonfiction book, I read an article published in the New Orleans' newspaper, *The Times-Democrat*, two days after the events detailed in *Shout So Hard to Heaven* came to an end. In an attempt to understand Robert Charles, the events' main character, the Sunday, 29 July 1900, issue of the newspaper carried the following headline on page three:

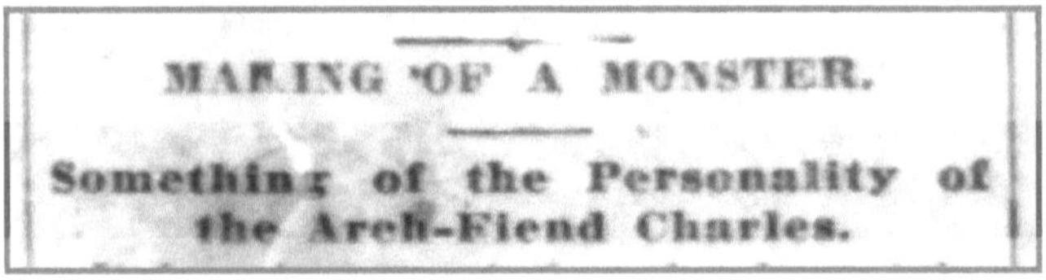
MAKING OF A MONSTER.

Something of the Personality of the Arch-Fiend Charles.

The article began with the following paragraph:

> What matter of a man was this fiend incarnate? What conditions developed him? Who were his preceptors? From what ancestral strain, if any, did he derive his ferocious hatred of whites, his cunning, his brute courage, the apostolic zeal he displayed in spreading the propaganda of African equality? These are questions involving one of the most remarkable psychological problems of modern times.[4]

The questions I asked after reading about Robert Charles were: What matter of a man was this intelligent, courageous, and diligent person? Who were the people and circumstances of his life that shaped a man who believed enough in himself and his worth that he would defend his life to the death? Why did he have such a strong belief that migration to Africa could give him the freedom he knew he deserved as a human being? It is not so much that these questions involve "one of the most remarkable psychological problems of modern times" as written in the 1900 article, but the questions of why white American citizens so persistently and strongly advocate their superiority over people who were black-skinned, even 120 years after the New Orleans race riot of 1900. This book also intends to show that Robert Charles was a man of intelligence and experience—not "cunning"—bravery and willingness to do what was right—not "brute courage"—and with a strong desire to enjoy democracy and all its opportunities—not "zeal [for] the propaganda of African equality."

Shout So Hard to Heaven: A Portrait of Robert Charles paints a more realistic and humane picture of this everyday, yet remarkable, man who just wanted to live a full, rich life but would not sacrifice his dignity and self-respect to do so.

— J.H. Clark

> "...in 1900 in New Orleans one of the most serious outbreaks of racial violence since Reconstruction occurred. At the center of the conflict was a remarkable man, until recently perhaps one of the most neglected historical figures in American race relations. His name was Robert Charles, and possibly he was the first fully self-conscious black militant in the United States."
>
> — Joel Williamson, Ph.D.,
> *The Crucible of Race*[5]

Mid-summer 1894, New Orleans

A young black man named Robert Charles, originally from Mississippi and new to this Louisiana city, went to work as usual in the steamy heat he woke up to each morning. He was building a life for himself—happy to be working and glad to have a place to live. He enjoyed socializing with friends and family, but he also was on a path of self improvement. Robert was a self-educated man, well read and knowledgeable in an array of subjects. He loved to read, even seeking out used textbooks to teach himself.

Even though blacks and whites had built a relatively good working relationship in New Orleans and other parts of the South during Reconstruction, over the next several years Robert grew concerned about how he saw blacks dehumanized, especially in a number of the New Orleans' newspapers he read. He knew too that throughout the South the number of black people lynched by white mobs grew at an alarming rate. He was particularly disturbed by the lynching of Sam Hose in 1899.

Upset by the way society suppressed blacks, Robert looked to the back-to-Africa movement as a possible solution to being free of the growing restraints his nation put on blacks. He saw moving to Africa as a chance to live without the intense fear he felt enveloped his very being on a day-to-day basis—the fear of being killed by whites based solely on their perceptions of him as a black man.

By the beginning of the twentieth century, race relations had deteriorated to such an extent that escalating racism and white violence toward blacks came crashing down on Robert and the entire city of New Orleans.

Chapter 1

Summer 1892, Mississippi

No way was that scarecrow doin' his job. That damn crow was just pick, pick, pickin' away at the straw that stuck here and there outta the scarecrow. That bird didn't give a damn. He wasn't scared at all. That nest he was a'buildin' would be the envy of all them other crows.

As the summer sun rose over the flat Louisiana countryside, the scarecrow that was supposed to be guarding the young corn was silhouetted against the orange-yellow sky. Another crow landed on the scarecrow's outstretched arms and picked hay from his leaning head intent on beating the first crow at his own game…declaring his superiority over this paradigm of a person.

An empty train track ran alongside the cornfield, running parallel to a dirt road. It underlined the quiet of this summer morning. But as the day brightened to reveal a cloudless azure sky, a folksy sung-out-loud tune with a hint of a spiritual and a smidgen of pioneering blues escorted Robert and Henry Charles into the scene. Deep, energetic voices matched their strong and robust pace.

"White folks all lend me your attention
I won't detain you long,
I'll tell you about de mancipation,
In this my simple song,
I was born way down in Louisiana
By my stile you can plainly see,
In dat sunny land I've hoed de cotton
My good ole wife and me,
Dey told us all de day was gwine to
come
And it filled my heart with glee,
Now white folks I still remember
The day I was sot free.
Oh! yes I'm free
And I'm happy you can see
Oh! yes I'm free
And I'm happy you can see."[6]

Robert, a strong, self-confident six-foot-tall 26-year-old man with medium-brown skin and broad shoulders, and his brother, Henry, 34, walked confidently along the railroad tracks. Robert carried a Civil War-era Springfield Model 1855 rifle slung over his left shoulder. Henry held a newer Winchester Model 1890 .22 long rifle through the crook of his right arm.

Robert saluted the scarecrow as he passed, startling and scaring away the crows, just as Henry started singing again. Robert picked it up, harmonizing to his brother's deep bass tones with his own tenor voice.

"Ise growing old and am quite feeble,
And my hair am turning gray,
But still I ever shall remember
What I head ole massa say,
Dar's gonna be a big commotion
Down in dat sunny land,
And all da darks on dis plantation
Would soon be a happy band,
De proclamation papers massa Lincoln
signed
In da year of sixty-three,
And I nebber shall forget no nebber
Da day I was sot free.
Oh! yes I'm free
And I'm happy you can see
Oh! yes I'm free
And I'm happy you can see."[6]

Both brothers grew quiet as they finished singing their song, but Robert seemed slightly bothered, a look his brother Henry knew well.

"What you thinkin' 'bout now, brother?" Henry asked.

Robert didn't answer for a minute. He stopped walking and turned to look at his older brother. "Have you ever wondered, Henry, what it was like for Mama and Pa when they weren't free?"

"I don't have to wonder, Robert," Henry said quietly. "I was born in slavery. Now, mind you, I was just knee-high to a grasshopper, but one of my first memories as a child…I think I was just about four…was a white man, I think the field foreman, comin' up to Mama as she was pickin' cotton. I was just a tot, sitting in the dirt playin' with a couple of rocks. The man came right up to Mama and asked her why I wasn't workin'. He was talkin' loud so I stopped playin' and looked up. He said, 'This monkey of yours is big enough now that he could be pickin'.' Ma, she stood her ground—that I remember—and she looked right at the man. 'He's just a little child,' she said. 'He's barely four years old.' 'Can he stand?' the man yelled. 'Can he walk? Can he pick a boll and put it in the basket? I'd say the answer to all them questions is yes!' The man, he took a step toward me and as he was bendin' down, I heard Pa shoutin' from across the field. All I heard was him shoutin' Ma's name. 'Mariah!' And he shouted, 'Mariah!' one more time. At that moment, Mama picked me up, shouted out loud to Pa, 'I got it, Jasper!' and she then turned straight at the man and said, and this I'll never forget, 'You touch my son, and I'll let the Misses know you harmed my child.' Ma, she was holding me so tight. Not a bit of her body was shakin', but I was so tight up against her and she held my head so tight to her chest, I could HEAR how fast her heart was beatin'. She knew what she said would get to the man. He stared her down, but then he just turned and walked away, startin' to yell at some other poor Negro in the field. And Mama, she just held on to me and whispered, 'Nobody's going to hurt you, baby boy. Mama and Pa got you covered.'"

Robert just looked at his brother. "Why haven't you ever told me this story, Henry?"

Henry smiled at his younger brother and placed his hand on Robert's sweating shoulder. "No need to, Robert. You was born in freedom, as Mamaalways used to say. 'He may have got his start in my belly while we were still slaves, but he was born to freedom.'"

Robert smiled at Henry and said, "Yeah, I remember her saying that to me whenever I'd get in trouble or go off looking for trouble. She'd grab each of my arms with both her hands, turn me directly to her and say, 'Robert, you were born to freedom, and you are NOT to do anything to mess that up!' I'd bow my head, and she'd have none of that!"

Both brothers laughed, with Henry remembering, "You're right. She'd have no shame on us. 'Look right into my eyes, boy!' she'd say."

Robert picked up the memory, "And she'd then say, 'Don't take freedom lightly. It's as serious as it comes. Your Pa and I worked too hard to bring this family into freedom, and you make sure you remain free.' I'd look right into her eyes and say, 'Yes, ma'am.'"

"And then Pa would pipe up," Henry said. "He'd always follow up Mama's proclamation of freedom with…"

Both brothers recited in unison, "'And just remember, a mule hooked to a plow don't mean he ain't free but the minute you chain him up at night, THAT'S the day you done took his freedom!'"

Both men laughed and started walking again. Henry noticed that Robert still had that look in his eyes that meant he was thinking through everything they had remembered. What he didn't know was that Robert had been thinking about his parents' talk of freedom since they first spoke to their children about this precious life. Robert still had mixed feelings about what freedom meant. He was proud that his Pa, born into slavery, had worked hard in freedom to buy a mule and plow. Yes, he still worked the white man's land on shares, but unlike so many other Negroes, he didn't have to pay rent for his work team. He kept more fruits of his labor. That was a taste of freedom. And his parents made sure he, Robert, got some schooling, even learning to read themselves, encouraging their son to keep on learning. That was freedom. But could they own land? Could he, Robert, speak openly to whites, especially a white woman, without fearing the feel of a rope around his neck? Over the past number of years, that fear was growing as fast as a radish after a good rain. Robert asked himself, "What will my freedom be?"

Robert and Henry reached the edge of a small town. Robert wiped his sweaty brow on the torn shirt hanging off his right shoulder and brought his attention and thoughts back to the here and now. Henry looked at Robert, who nodded to his brother.

They continued walking into town along the rails. A few white clapboard houses stood with fenced yards backed up against the train tracks. As they passed the third house, Robert and Henry saw a white man in dungarees scattering seed to his chickens under several tall pecan trees at the side of his house. The man's face was wrinkled and bronzed from years of working in the blazing sun.

A boy, shirtless under his overalls, carried a slop bucket to the hogs penned up in the mucky sty to the side of an unpainted wooden outbuilding. A middle-aged woman with gray-streaked hair tied up in a bandana hung laundry on the side-yard clothesline. Her sleeveless, faded cotton dress whipped around her ankles in the growing breeze.

The sun, now fully above the horizon, shone its light and heat directly on the clear day. The three members of this white family slowed their work and glanced at Robert and Henry as they walked past the house along the tracks. Only the man, Mitch, showed any concern. His wife, Janie, went about her business hanging clothes on the line, and grandson Tommie went back to tossing slop to the pigs.

Mitch set down the seed bucket, stood up straight, and put his hands on his hips while turning to watch the brothers pass. Keeping his eyes on them, Mitch shouted to his wife, “Go on in the house, Janie!”

About ten feet past the house, Robert and Henry stopped walking and looked back over their shoulders when they heard Mitch’s shout.

Janie continued clipping her clothes to the line, shouting back to her husband, “I’m almost done with the wash, Mitch.”

“Get in the house right now, woman! And you too, Tommie!” Mitch yelled with authority, hands on hips.

Janie picked up her half-empty wicker basket and walked quickly into the backyard. Tommie, throwing the empty bucket on the ground, ran after his grandma while glancing with a mix of fear and curiosity at his grandpa.

Robert and Henry turned away showing little concern. They continued their trek away from the house and into town. The brothers reached the train station about ten minutes later. An engine with a stretch of boxcars stood parallel to the depot, ready to be loaded. The engine bore the name Louisville, New Orleans and Texas Railroad on its side. Robert and Henry stepped off the tracks and walked to the loading platform. A sign on a post at the entrance to the platform read *Rolling Fork.*

A tall, skinny black 15-year-old, Beanpole, worked with a middle-aged black man, Carter. They loaded hay into the fourth boxcar down from the engine. Robert and Henry approached.

Robert raised his voice and called out, “Hey, Beanpole!”

Beanpole glanced up and then turned back to his work without speaking.

Robert reached him and took hold of Beanpole’s shoulder, turning the teenager toward him. “Do you have my Colt?” Robert asked.

“Brakeman took it,” Beanpole answered quickly, pointing in the direction of the train’s engine.

Henry stood behind and off to the side of Robert, keeping his eyes on Carter. Robert looked in the direction Beanpole pointed. He saw Brakeman, a 46-year-old white man dressed in a rail worker’s uniform, standing alongside the train’s engine. Robert and Henry, cradling their rifles in their arms and standing up straighter, stepped around the bales of hay closest to the depot and strode toward Brakeman.

As the brothers passed Carter, he spoke with warning to Robert and Henry, "Best be careful of him."

Brakeman, not fully aware of what was happening, knelt next to the engine as he inspected the train's drive wheel.

Robert shouted out, "Brakeman!"

Brakeman looked up and stopped what he was doing.

Robert yelled, "I've come for my Colt."

Brakeman stood and ran to the open box car attached to the engine. He swung himself up into the car as Robert and Henry approached. "Stay away from me!" Brakeman shouted. "I ain't got nothin' of yours!"

Henry moved toward the boxcar, but Robert pulled him back as he saw Brakeman reach under his jacket and bring out the Colt.

Brakeman aimed the Colt .45 Peacemaker pistol at Robert and fired. Robert and Henry dove behind bales of hay and took positions to return fire. Beanpole and Carter crouched behind the bales staying as low as possible.

The station clerk, alerted by the gunfire, looked out his ticket window and promptly slammed the wooden shutters closed. He dashed into the train station lobby, shouting at three white men and a boy looking out the window at the commotion.

"All y'all, git away from them windows," he yelled.

At the sound of another shot, a stray bullet shattered the glass at the top of the window. The men and boy scrambled to get away. The youngest man grabbed the boy by the waist and threw him to the floor.

Back on the platform, Brakeman fired two more shots at Robert and Henry, missing. Henry, squatting on one knee with his back to the haystacks, aimed his Winchester at the open depot door, keeping watch in that direction.

Beanpole hunched between Henry and Robert with both knees pulled in tight against his chest. He hugged them close with his skinny arms. He looked from Robert to Henry and back to Robert, who was in position to fire in Brakeman's direction.

Robert looked down the barrel of his rifle aiming straight for Brakeman's heart. As he began to pull the trigger, he shifted his aim slightly higher. The bullet sent Brakeman's cap flying.

Startled, Brakeman hurled himself to his left onto the boxcar bed, out of Robert's sight. Brakeman's booted foot showed slightly at the bottom of the boxcar's open door. Robert took aim and fired, striking the floor just beside Brakeman's foot. The foot disappeared from the opening as Brakeman shouted from inside the boxcar.

"Stop shooting!" he implored Robert.

Robert cautiously looked over the bale—his rifle still poised—and watched as Brakeman's right hand slowly came into view through the boxcar's door. He held the Colt by the muzzle.

"Hold your fire," Brakeman shouted. "You can have your damn fool gun!"

Brakeman tossed the Colt onto the platform and quickly drew his hand back into the boxcar.

Robert, laughing and nudging a shaking Beanpole, said to the teen, "Go get it for me, Scairdy Cat. I'll keep you covered."

Beanpole crawled out from behind the hay and took a racing start toward the pistol. He grabbed the gun and headed back to the hay, slipping and falling on the way. Once safely behind the bale, Beanpole handed the gun to Robert, who took hold of the Colt with a bandana-covered hand. Before touching it, Robert thoroughly rubbed the Colt with the cloth. After a good polish, he held the Colt lovingly in his bare hands and spoke to Beanpole.

"Thanks, kid," he said with a smile and a wink. "We'll make a man out of you yet." Turning to Henry, Robert said, "Come on, brother. It's time to blow this town."

Robert and Henry stood and walked off the platform. Henry faced forward, keeping his eyes on the area in front of the train. Robert stepped backward, covering the depot. They held their rifles poised and ready for trouble.

A small gathering had formed along the road leading to the depot, but no one made a move toward the two armed men. Robert and Henry worked their way past the few houses leading out of town. Once Robert was sure no one was following, he turned away from Rolling Fork. Both men ran, looking over their shoulders frequently.

A few more white men, along with several teenage boys, joined the small group on the road outside the depot. Brakeman stepped up to the group and grabbed one of the boys, Matt, by his arm.

"Hightail it down to Sheriff Yates, Matt, and tell him two crazy niggers 'bout killed me." When Matt didn't make a move, Brakeman shouted at him, "Well, don't just stand there gawkin', boy, go on!"

Matt turned quickly and ran off in the direction of the sheriff's office on the other side of the town.

Robert and Henry kept running until they came to a fork. They chose the left-hand bend in the road, which they knew would get them out of the town's sight. They slowed down to a walk once 'round the bend. Without haste but breathing heavily, the brothers stepped off the road and headed into the piney woods to their left.

They came upon two horses tied to a tree. Robert and Henry untied their mounts and led them farther into the trees and onto a path. The men swung themselves up on the horses' bare backs, took the reins made of rope in their hands, and rode at a fair clip deeper into the woods, finally emerging in a meadow.

The brothers and their steeds raced across the meadow and jumped the fence at the far side, ending up on another small dirt road. They rode a short distance before stopping. They dismounted and led their horses to a cluster of large grayish ironstone and sandstone rocks. They wrapped the horses' reins around the sturdiest branch of a nearby tree.

Along the road Robert and Henry had taken out of town, a small posse made up of the sheriff, his deputy, and two of the townsmen that had been outside the depot rode their horses at a gallop down the road, going straight and not taking the bend that Robert and Henry had followed.

The brothers sat with their backs against the rocks, wiping their sweaty faces with bandanas. Tension remained clear on their faces, but when they looked at one another for a couple of seconds, they relaxed and burst out laughing.

"Remind me to say I'm busy next time you ask a favor," Henry half joked to Robert.

Robert grinned and shook his head. "I should've known better than to leave the Colt with Beanpole. He probably went showing it off until Brakeman caught sight of it."

"Yeah," Henry agreed. "And ya know what happens when that son-of-a-bitch takes a fancy to somethin'. No doubt he leaned pretty hard on 'Pole." Both men were quiet for a moment and Henry grew more serious. He said hesitantly, "Ya think Beanpole'll be okay?"

Robert smiled gently at his brother and placed his hand on Henry's shoulder. "Henry, you're just like Mama," he said. "You worry too much."

Henry remained serious. "Robert, this county won't be safe for a while. And we'll both have to quit the railroad."

Nodding in agreement but looking away, Robert said, "We need to be moving on anyway. Four years is a long time to be working on the tracks. You have anything in mind?"

"Pa's been askin' me to come back and help with the sharecroppin' out on Halloway's cotton crops," Henry answered. "Now that Lizabeth's expecting, I think it'd be a good idea."

"Back to Copiah?" Robert asked without much enthusiasm. After a hesitation, he said, "I guess I could farm a few months…if Pa needs a hand."

Henry reached out and turned Robert back to look him in the face. "Me, Robert, not you," he said with big-brother authority. "We've got to split up. They'll be lookin' for two Negro brothers last name of Charles. Besides, there's nothin' for you back in Copiah County."

With the barest hint of a smile and a shy twinkle in his eyes, Robert looked at Henry and said, "There's Lovinia. Right?"

Henry threw his head back and laughed out loud. "That's true, but, brother," he mockingly warned, "you'd be sharin' her with Louie Hanson."

Robert furrowed his brow in mock seriousness and said in a feigned 'country' accent, "What 'cha talkin' 'bout, Henry?"

Henry smiled at his younger brother and said, "Don't play stupid with me, Robert. You know them two been havin' at it for a time now. Wouldn't surprise me one little bit if a Louis Jr. or little Liza Mae joins their family in six months or so."

Both brothers laughed before Henry turned serious again. "Things are tough all over right now, Robert," Henry said, "especially for us Negroes. But you're special, Robert. You got learnin' and a good way with words. This ain't the place for you to be. Didn't you tell me somethin' once about New Orleans?"

"Yeah," Robert responded with a bit of doubt. "But I don't know. Maybe I should head back to Vicksburg."

Henry urged his brother, "Mama and Pa'll be real proud of you, Robert, when you make a life for yourself in New Orleans."

Despite feeling a hint of excitement, Robert expressed his concern. "You won't worry them with the shooting, will you?" Robert asked Henry. "Just tell them I decided to move on. And I'll let y'all know when I'm settled."

"Sure," Henry agreed, "but now we best be movin' on."

"Wait a sec!" Robert said suddenly.

"What?" Henry asked.

"You know that metal lock box in my room under the bed?" Robert asked. "Wrap it up, will you? Make it look like an ordinary package. I'll let you know where I'm staying and you can send it on to me. It has all the money I've saved while working for the railroad."

"Sure, Robert," Henry answered. "Just let me know where to send it."

Robert took a small key from his pants' pocket and handed it to Henry. "Before you wrap it up," he said to Henry with a smile, "take a few dollars out for yourself, Elizabeth, and the baby."

Henry refused the key. "I can't do that. It's your money. You earned it."

Robert held the key out to his brother and spoke with more muscle in his voice. "Take it!" he commanded, before softening his tone. "Consider it my present to the baby. Say it's from Uncle Robert."

Henry laughed and took the key Robert offered him. "No doubt you'll want that baby named for you," he said. "I'll consider it if we have ourselves a son, but there ain't no way Lizabeth and me namin' no girl Roberta!"

Robert and Henry stood, both laughing and shaking their heads. Henry picked up his Winchester and handed it to Robert. "Here," he said. "Take my Winchester and you give me yours. A big city man like you deserves to be carryin' a decent rifle."

Robert laughed more quietly and shook his head, accepting the Winchester and handing Henry his Springfield rifle. "Thanks, Henry," he said seriously, extending his right hand to his brother.

Henry took hold of Robert's outstretched hand to shake it, smiled, and pulled Robert to him. The brothers hugged tightly for a moment then released each other. The men walked to their horses, unlooped the reins from the branch that held them, and swung up on their mounts.

Once settled on his steed's back, Henry reminded Robert, "Let me know where to send your stuff. And, Robert…"

"Yeah?"

"You might wanna use another name for the time being," Henry advised his younger brother. "They be lookin' for the nigger who pulled that trigger."

The men threw back their heads and guffawed. Robert turned his mount away from Henry, who headed back in the direction of home in Copiah County, Mississippi. Robert headed west. Riding away from each other, they both started singing the song they voiced earlier that day. But unlike the melodious tune they sang that morning, their two songs were out of sync—no harmony at all.

As Robert rode along solo on the Mississippi country road, his singing became more upbeat as the lyrics of the first song made way for a new tune.

In the evening by the moonlight
You could hear banjos ringing
In the evening by the moonlight
You could hear my folks all singing
How my mother she would enjoy it
She would sit all night and listen

As we sang in the evening by the
moonlight oh yeah.[7]

As the sky grew dusky, Robert approached a livery stable. An older white man, working outside the stable, asked, "What can I do you for? Need a stable for the night?"

"I hate to do it, but I'm needing to sell this fellow," Robert answered.

He dismounted and led his horse by the reins to the stable owner, who gave the horse a thorough going over. He ran his hands along the mount's flanks, lifted each hoof, and made sure the teeth were healthy.

"Looks like a good one to me," the man told Robert. "And I'm down a mount. I can take him off your hands for thirty dollars."

"He's great as a mount, and he can pull a small cart along at a good pace," Robert said, talking up his horse. "A guy in New Orleans offered me fifty bucks for him."

The man laughed, "No doubt you could get fifty for him in the city, but the best I can do you for is thirty."

"Make it forty," Robert responded, "and you got yourself one fine animal."

"My final offer is thirty-five," the man stated.

"Deal," Robert agreed.

The man stepped into a small sideroom he used as his office and came back outside holding a ledger book. "I keep records of all transactions," he said.

"Of course," Robert agreed.

"So what's your name?" the man asked, his hand poised to write in the ledger.

Robert hesitated for a brief moment then said confidently, "Curtis Robertson. But my friends call me Buster."

"Well, Buster," the man said, handing several bills and a few coins to Robert, "here's your money." The man counted out the money into Robert's outstretched hand before taking the offered ropes.

Robert stroked the horse's neck with a loving good-bye to his faithful mount. "I'll miss you, ya old fool," Robert said, pocketing the money.

Two years later, in 1894, Robert walked along Canal Street, which ran along the upriver side of the French Quarter in New Orleans. Horse-drawn wagons and the occasional car rolled past him. He looked at the traffic and the people around him with a smile. He had a job and a roof over his head. He added about a book a month to his collection, reading up on new subjects with enthusiasm. He recently had read about a movement to migrate to Africa. That caught his attention. Robert Charles was home.

Chapter 2

Evening, Friday, 13 July 1900, New Orleans

Robert hurried along Canal Street, where many of the horse-drawn wagons had been replaced by automobiles, among them a few of the nation's first mass-produced cars, the 1900 Oldsmobile. Street cars clanged along just as they did six years earlier, but many more businesses and people made the street much busier.

Now 34 years old, Robert was dressed in a nice-fitting suit with a vest, stiff-collared shirt, showy tie, polished shoes, and a bowler hat that was the envy of his friends. The contrast to the dusty dungarees and workman's shirt he wore back in the summer of 1892 was significant, but the look of confidence and intelligence that most everyone noticed when first meeting Robert was much the same. The look was enhanced with life experience, not to mention his stylish moustache.

Robert had returned to his room after his day's work at the sawmill to clean up and change. He hoped to have an entertaining Friday evening at a music club listening to Charles "Buddy" Bolton play his jazzy coronet with three other musicians—one on a trombone, one playing a clarinet, and a guitarist keeping the jazzy, bluesy rhythm to this new improvised style of music.

Robert entered the club, took off his hat, and approached the bar, habitually tugging at the ends of his waxed moustache with his right thumb and forefinger. He motioned to the bartender, who poured Robert a shot of whiskey. Robert emptied the glass in one swallow then wiped his mouth with the back of his hand, smoothing out his moustache. He walked over to a round table where Can Can Jimmie, Hollering John, Deadeye Dick, and Ruby sat. Ruby, an attractive 38-year-old light-skinned Creole woman, sat next to Hollering John, an older black man. Dressed in a silky red gown and adorned with a crystal necklace, earrings, and bracelet, Ruby draped her left arm around Hollering's shoulders.

Across the table, Can Can Jimmie, a darker black man about Robert's age, caught sight of his friend approaching the table. Smiling, Can Can said with a wave of his arm, "Robert! Join us, man!"

Robert greeted Can Can Jimmie and Deadeye Dick, a slender middle-aged black man, with a handshake before he nodded at Ruby with a slight smile on his lips. Deadeye Dick scooted his chair a little to the side to make room for Robert to sit. Robert reached across the table and shook Hollering John's hand before he sat down next to Deadeye.

"It's been a long time, John," Robert said.

"Too long," Hollering replied. "We was just talkin' 'bout you. Noticed you at the bar. At least Ruby did. She's been asking after you." Hollering John nudged Ruby and chuckled.

Ruby smiled at Robert and said with mock chastisement, "Now, John, don't embarrass Robert." She said to Robert nonchalantly, "I was just wondering why you haven't been around for a while."

Robert smiled back, "I'm here now." He took a small folded newspaper from his coat pocket and placed it on the table.

Deadeye picked it up, reading the title out loud, "*Voice of Missions*." Deadeye looked up at Robert then scanned the printing on the newspaper's cover. "What's this?" he asked. "Who's Bishop Turner?"

"He's a bishop with the AME church in Atlanta," Robert answered. "He preaches about emigrating to Africa among other issues."

"It says here," Deadeye said, "that Bishop Turner has been setting up churches in Africa."

"He's been to Africa many times," Robert said. "As a matter of fact, he's also made it possible for lots of South Africans to come to college over here in the States. I really admire how he's combined his missionary work with promoting the education and advancement of Negroes both here and in Africa."

"I've heard that not everyone in his church is happy with that," Ruby said.

Robert looked up, a bit surprised. "That's true," he agreed. "But if he's anything, Bishop Henry Turner is his own man." Robert paused and looked at Ruby. He could see an interest in her eyes he hadn't noticed before. He went on sharing his thoughts about the Bishop. "I remember reading about how Bishop Turner, speaking at the first Black Baptist Convention, chastised people, even blacks, who thought their God was some blue-eyed, blond-haired, crooked-nose white man."

Can Can, Deadeye, and Hollering laughed at this description. Ruby just listened.

Robert continued, “I think the Bishop is right. Why can’t our God be in our image, especially if we’re supposed to be made in His? I’ve been reading about Africa before we got brought over here as slaves. Tribes all the way back to the beginning of time created art, statues, and writings where their gods resemble themselves. As Bishop Turner said, ‘and why should not the Negro believe that he resembles God.’”

No one spoke for a moment until Hollering John broke the silence. “You still sellin’ them newspapers, Buster?” Hollering asked, using the name Robert went by when they met, which was right after Robert settled in New Orleans.

“That’s right,” Robert confirmed. “Are you interested?”

“Me?” Hollering said loudly while laughing. “Nooo, sirrie. I’d be buyin’ into trouble.”

Deadeye had continued to read the newspaper, and he looked up and addressed his friends. “It says here there’s a pamphlet called ‘What a Colored Man Should Do to Vote’,” he read.

“Last time I tried to vote in Mississippi was three years ago,” Can Can pitched in. “’Bout got myself kilt,” he remembered, speaking a bit more quietly.

Hollering John leaned in and put his elbows on the table before telling the group, “I never forgot goin‘ with my daddy the first time he voted. He worked all them years as a slave and now he was gettin‘ to vote,” Hollering said, putting a lot of emphasis on the word ‘vote’. He continued, “I felt prouder’n a hen-house rooster! Couldn’t wait for the day I came of age.”

“Me too,” agreed Can Can. “But given a choice ’tween the vote and one more day of livin’…well, there ain’t no choice.”

Robert placed both hands firmly on the table top. “That’s just the point, Jimmie,” Robert urged. “We shouldn’t have to choose. We should have both.”

Shaking his head, Hollering John dismissed what Robert had said. “There’s a long way ’tween ‘should have’ and ‘got’, son. The price of the ticket is just too high.”

Robert’s face muscles tightened. He clasped his hands trying to control his growing anger. “But someone has to pay it,” Robert declared. “It’s just that attitude, John, that keeps us at the bottom.”

“Son,” Hollering replied in a quieter, calmer voice but insisting on respect, “you best hold your tongue. You may be younger and stronger, but I got a few moves left in me that might surprise ya.”

Still angry, Robert stood up from the table, pushing his chair back with force. “If you will excuse me,” he said, looking down at Deadeye Dick. “Dick, my newspaper, please.”

Deadeye folded the *Voice* and handed it to Robert, who grabbed the paper and turned away from the table. A young black man, Lewis Forstall, got up from a table next to the one where Robert had been sitting and grabbed Robert’s left arm from behind.

Robert whirled around with a dangerous look on his face and both hands as hard fists, causing Lewis to freeze in his tracks. When Robert realized that no danger threatened him, his face and body relaxed, but not before admonishing Lewis. “You’re putting one foot in the grave when you grab a man from behind like that,” he said sternly.

Lewis responded timidly. “I’m sorry. I…I just wanted to ask you something.”

“Ask me what?”

“About that newspaper I heard you talking about,” Lewis answered. “I’d like to subscribe.”

Robert’s stance and tone relaxed a bit, but he remained serious. He said to Lewis, “Let’s move over to the bar.”

Robert led the way, and when he reached the bar, he took a small notebook and pen out of his jacket pocket. “What’s your name?” Robert asked Lewis while writing in his notebook.

“Forstall, Lewis Forstall,” he answered. “There’s no ‘e’ in Forstall, and it’s Lewis with a ‘w’.”

Robert made sure he had Lewis’s name spelled correctly then said, “It’s a nickel an issue. How many issues can you afford?”

“Two, I guess,” Lewis responded. “Just to start with.”

“That’s fine,” Robert assured Lewis. “When you can afford more, just let me know. You’ll see me around. Now, what’s your address?”

“Ten-eighty-five A, Saratoga Street. Here in New Orleans.”

Robert wrote the address under Lewis’s name. As he closed the notebook and put it back in his pocket, he confirmed, “Okay. I’ve got you down for two issues so it's ten cents. They come out once a month, and you'll get your first issue in early August."

Lewis dug into his right-hand pants' pocket and brought out a handful of change. He picked through the coins and handed Robert two nickels. Robert pocketed the money.

"The newspapers will be mailed to you," he told Lewis.

Robert seemed to be wrapping up their conversation, but after a hesitation he said to Lewis, "By the way, you might be interested in coming to a meeting next Wednesday evening at the Union Sons' Hall before the dancing starts."

"What kind of meeting?" Lewis asked without much enthusiasm.

Robert hesitated before speaking, looking around to see if anybody was listening. He turned back to Lewis and said quietly, "We'll be talking about our right to vote and Africa."

Lewis's response surprised Robert. Smiling and extending his hand to Robert, Lewis said, "Thanks. I'll be there." The men shook hands.

The confident young man walked away from Robert and the bar, heading toward the front door. A middle-aged white man, Harold Carruthers, had been watching Robert and Lewis from a corner of the bar. As Lewis left, Carruthers got up from his table and approached Robert.

"Could I have a word with you?" Carruthers asked with just enough authority to concern Robert.

Robert stated cautiously, "I'm listening."

Carruthers motioned to an empty table at the back of the bar. "Let's move over to that table back there…where we can have some privacy," he said.

Carruthers and Robert moved to a secluded table at the back of the club. Robert stood behind the seat nearest the back door and waited to sit. Once Carruthers sat down, Robert did as well.

Carruthers continued, "I'm Harold Carruthers, manager and part owner of this club," he told Robert. "I'd like to know what you were just doing."

Robert kept his arms at his side and his chair backed away from the table. He looked directly at Carruthers when he spoke. "I told that young man about a dance tomorrow night," he stated calmly and definitively.

Carruthers crossed his arms and leaned back in his chair while holding Robert's gaze. "I saw money change hands," he declared. "Now, I'll admit that's all I saw pass between the two of you, but you may have slipped him something without me seeing it."

Robert stared at Carruthers for a moment without responding or breaking his direct eye contact. "Are you accusing me of selling something I shouldn't have?" he asked Carruthers.

"I'm telling you what I saw, and, to be honest, it didn't look like the kind of business I want in this club," Carruthers answered.

"Well, I'm glad we can be honest with each other," Robert continued, "because the only business I have in this club is buying your whiskey."

Ignoring this statement, Carruthers kept the conversation going in an accusatory direction. "I saw you earlier at a table with some people…showing them a newspaper."

Robert was beginning to steam inside, but he knew how to keep his cool. "You certainly seem to be doing a lot of watching," he observed.

"That's my job, and I want to know about yours," Carruthers insisted.

Using every ounce of energy to keep his voice even, Robert said, "I don't see that it's any of your business as long as my money's good, which it is."

Carruthers gripped the table's edge with both hands, leaned forward, and spoke more harshly and with the deliberate tone of finality in his voice. "Anything and everything that goes on in this club is my business," he said, then demanded, "Show me that newspaper!"

Robert looked directly at Carruthers for a second while taking a deep, imperceptible breath. He removed the newspaper from his coat pocket and tossed it on the table in front of Carruthers, who picked up the newspaper and glanced over the front cover. He threw the newspaper back on the table.

"I don't think this is the kind of reading material we want around here," he said. "Is this what you were selling that boy?"

"Yes," Robert answered without hesitation.

Carruthers put the sound of a threat in his voice when he told Robert, "I'd strongly recommend that you keep your business out of ours. A newspaper like this one means trouble, and the other owners of this place don't take kindly to troublemakers."

Without backing down an inch, Robert responded, "I don't see that I've caused any trouble. These people here keep your pockets lined. The few cents I get from them doesn't take any away from you."

"I'm not sure I like your attitude," Carruthers stated, determined to have the last word. "You best keep clear of this club in the future. There's no place for you here."

Robert reached for his newspaper and stood up suddenly. His quick movement caught Carruthers by surprise, causing him to spring to his feet and grip the table's edge tightly.

Shrugging, Robert said, "If not here, Carruthers, then someplace else." Robert folded the newspaper and placed it back in his coat pocket. He looked directly at Carruthers and spoke boldly, "There are places in this fine city of ours that you and your buddies can't touch."

Robert strode toward the bar's back door with his shoulders squared. Just before stepping outside, he turned to look at Carruthers, who had a dangerous, if slightly confused, look on his face.

Robert gave Carruthers a three-finger salute, turned, and exited.

Once outside, Robert's shoulders sagged slightly, as though the weight of another conflict with a white man and the injustice it represented was too much for him this night. He had looked forward to a fun night of music and friends. "What happened?" he asked himself. Robert stood still for a moment, knowing exactly what had happened. It was getting harder for Robert to step back from even the gentlest of confrontations, especially when it had to do with reaching his goal—building a free life in Africa. He knew it could happen, and arguing with other Negroes about this goal didn't bother him so much. It was the anger that spilled over when denied respect, such as with Carruthers. Robert believed he had a handle on that anger because it couldn't touch what he knew to be true. Despite what a white man may think about him, it was not who he was.

Robert stood and watched the street scene for a moment. It was alive with nightlife. Strains of music filled the night with a strange improvisation. Outside a red-lighted house, light-skinned Creole women dressed in alluring costumes of feathers, silk, and lace talked to white men in evening clothes as they walked past. Occasionally a man stopped and escorted a woman into the house. Other men, less well-dressed, left the bars and staggered down the street. There was much laughter and commotion when a drunken man tried to kiss one of the women, and she punched him in the mouth. As Robert turned to walk home, Ruby came out of the club.

"Robert," she called.

Robert turned around and said, "Ruby." He nodded in the direction of the red-lighted house, "Working tonight?" he asked.

Ruby seemed fine with the question. "Not tonight," she answered. Ruby smiled at Robert for a moment. "I'm glad I caught you. I thought…" She paused before saying, "It's John. He's sorry about upsetting you. I'd like to explain…"

"There's no need," Robert said smiling. "Really. I'm the one who's sorry," he tried to reassure her.

"You hit a nerve with him," Ruby continued. "Now he's embarrassed. He won't let it alone until he knows everything's straight with you again. Please… We could go across the street to my apartment. I'll fix us a drink."

Robert, opening his heart and widening his smile, stated, "Guess I can't refuse that offer."

Robert and Ruby crossed the street and walked past another bar. Ruby turned into an alley alongside the nightclub and led Robert to a set of stairs halfway down the dark passageway.

"Careful of that step. It's loose," she warned as Robert stepped over a broken plank.

When they reached the small landing at the top of the stairs, Ruby unlocked the door. "Wait here while I get us some light," she directed Robert as she stepped into her apartment.

Robert stood in the doorway as Ruby entered the sitting room and turned on a lamp. The room was cluttered with mementoes of Ruby's life. It gave the appearance of faded elegance. Some of her possessions obviously were expensive while others were keepsakes from the childhood she had spent with her grandmother. A vase, with a few chips along its rim, held a bunch of wilting flowers. Ruby quickly removed the stalks and tossed them in a waste basket.

Robert entered the room when Ruby motioned him in. He sat down on a small red settee, feeling a bit uncomfortable. He picked up a floral-patterned arm cushion and put it in his lap, crossing his arms atop the pillow. A few seconds later he looked down at his arms, uncrossed them, and replaced the pillow to his left. His ever-so-slight nervousness was lost on Ruby, who was busy at the sideboard. It was cluttered with various bottles of liquor and cut-crystal glasses.

Her back still to Robert, Ruby placed her hands on her hips, looked down at the sideboard and asked herself, "Now where is it?"

"Where's what?" Robert asked, looking up at Ruby and starting to feel more comfortable.

Ruby looked over her right shoulder at Robert, smiled, and answered, "That bottle of scotch I keep special for you."

Ruby turned back to the sideboard. She squatted and opened the door of the liquor cabinet. Ruby reached in the open cabinet and took out a three-quarters-full bottle of scotch. She closed the cabinet door and stood up again. Ruby poured two drinks, picked up a glass in each hand, turned around, and took a few steps over to the settee. She handed the drink to Robert as he stood up. They clinked glasses. Each took a sip, and Ruby put her glass down on the small coffee table in front of the settee.

She asked Robert, "Will you excuse me for a minute? I want to get out of my working clothes."

Robert continued to hold the glass of scotch in his right hand and gave Ruby a slight smile and nod of the head. Ruby went into the bedroom to her left. While she was gone, Robert looked around the sitting room. He picked up an old black-and-white photograph in a dark, hand-carved wooden frame that sat on the end table to his left. It was a picture of Hollering John when he was younger with a boy who looked to be about fifteen years old standing next to him. They were both smiling and looked happy to be together.

Ruby walked back into the sitting room wearing a red-and-purple Japanese kimono robe that offset the beauty of her slightly slanted dark-brown eyes. She also wore a single ruby-and-diamond ring on the fourth finger of her right hand. Robert hadn't noticed it earlier, probably hidden by the bling of her earlier jewelry and flashy dress.

Ruby picked up her drink from the coffee table, turned to her right, and moved to one of the two chairs adjacent to the settee. She sat and smiled across to Robert, who sat back down.

Ruby nodded at the picture Robert held. "You should've known John then," she said. "He was a lot like you—ready to take on the world single-handed."

Robert set the picture back down on the end table and paused before looking directly at Ruby. He said quietly but with a smidge of defiance, "I'm not out looking for trouble."

Ruby held Robert's eyes. "Neither was John…but he wanted his due."

Robert sighed and dropped his shoulders back against the settee, all the while holding Ruby's look. "Listen, Ruby," he began. "I was wrong to say those things to John."

Ruby didn't back down. "Yes, you were, Robert." Ruby paused then said, "I haven't always done right by him either. When John and I came to New Orleans, I was just a kid of fifteen. He took me away from a bad situation after my grandma passed, and I owe him a lot. Robert, he's paid the price, for him and me both."

Even though he wasn't quite sure what Ruby wanted to hear, Robert came out with the only response that seemed real to him. "I guess we all pay one way or another."

Ruby held Robert's look for just a moment before relaxing her body and glancing away briefly. As she looked back at this handsome man whose company she had always enjoyed, Ruby said, "That's the truth. But most of us only lose a part of ourselves. Take away pride or dignity—or even sprinkle in a bit of shame—and we can still find a way to manage."

Robert tried to interrupt Ruby, but she continued without hesitation.

"It's nothing compared to what that man suffered. He didn't go looking for trouble either. It found him. All he wanted was for people to take notice of him. They noticed John all right, and he paid for the privilege with his son's life. That was too much for John. Too much for any parent to suffer."

A chill ran through Robert's body, and he responded in barely a whisper, "I didn't know."

"There's lots of stories like John's that we don't know," Ruby said with all the truth of people's histories wrapped up in that one statement.

After almost a full ten seconds of silence, where Robert could only imagine what horror John and his family had endured, Robert decided to change the conversation's tone by stating, "Tell me yours."

Ruby laughed, stood, and walked to the window across from the settee to open it as she said, "It's like most stories. Make you laugh one minute and cry the next. I just hope my last chapter has me laughing."

As she opened the window, the music from the club below filled the room. Ruby stood looking out the window and listened. Robert stayed seated on the settee, keeping his eyes on this beautifully complex woman.

The music that came from below carried the rich, husky voice of a female singer accompanied by a bluesy jazz piano.

"...Tout ça, vois-tu, ça n'me fait rien
C'qui m'paralyse
C'est qu'i faut qu'on coupe, avant l'mien
L'col de ma ch'mise
En pensant au froid des ciseaux
A la toilette
J'ai peur d'avoir froid dans les os...

Voices of the club's patrons joined in the singing of the last line of this verse, sending the lyrics more clearly into Ruby's apartment.

A la Roquette.

The woman started singing alone again, partnered only with the piano's tinkling melody.

Aussi j'vas raidir pour marcher
Sans qu'ça m'émeuve

C'est pas moi que j'voulais flancher
Devant la veuve
J'veux pas qu'on dise que j'ai eu l'trac
De la lunette
Avant d'éternuer dans l'sac

Again, the voices of the club's patrons rallied on the last line of the song, this time with Ruby quietly singing out loud as well.

A la Roquette.[8]

At the song's end, Ruby turned away from the window, walked to the settee, picked up both glasses off the coffee table, and went to the sideboard to refresh the drinks. She turned back to Robert and handed him his glass. He took it from her and sipped while looking up at Ruby.

Robert picked up their conversation where they had left off. "No thoughts for the future? No dreams?" he asked.

Ruby laughed with a hint of bitterness. "See that jar up on the mantle," she said, nodding to the shelf above the bricked-up fireplace. "I'm keeping my dreams sealed up tight in there. That way they can't get at me. No expectations, no disappointments."

Robert, regretting that he had asked the question and fearing he'd embarrassed Ruby, tried to think of how to respond. He saw in Ruby's face the steadfast look of a survivor who has seen and experienced life in a way he never would know. Robert realized just how different they were as individuals.

Without thinking anymore that he might be offending or hurting Ruby, Robert stated, "That's all that keeps me going, thinking about where I'll be someday. Soon, I hope."

Ruby, knowing just how to make another person feel more comfortable while tucking away her own pain, put the shine of the moment back on Robert. "Africa?" she asked.

Robert sensed that the mood—or perhaps the nature of their relationship to one another—had shifted significantly. "That's right," he answered quietly.

Ruby, still standing, walked over to Robert and placed herself directly in front of him. She held out both her hands to him, and Robert took hold of them and stood without any doubts. The two were in exactly the same moment, knowing that each could be the other's savior, even if just for this one point in time.

Ruby let go of Robert's hands as she stood directly in front of him. She smoothed his jacket's lapels and said with acceptance and love, "You keep on dreaming, Robert. Maybe it'll be enough for both of us. But for now, just stay with me and make tonight important."

In the intimacy of her bedroom, Ruby untied her kimono's sash and let the silk robe slide down to expose her bare shoulders. When she sat on the bed, the kimono slipped fully away showing her beautiful and beguiling body. She reached up for Robert's hand and pulled him down onto the bed, helping him remove the restraints of jacket, vest, fully buttoned shirt, and all the other wrappings in which Robert liked to display an important part of how he saw himself.

Their sex was full of passion and fury, with respect for each other but little love, as though they were fighting to make their encounter more than it was while at the same time making the most of what they had at that moment.

Morning, Saturday, 14 July 1900, New Orleans

Dawn's first light was accompanied by a rooster crowing out in the neighborhood and the shop workers heading out to ready New Orleans for the day to come.

Robert sat up and got out of bed while Ruby continued to sleep. He dressed quickly, draping his vest over his arm and leaving off the adornment of tie, collar stays, and cufflinks. He left Ruby's apartment without waking her.

Robert exited the alley beside Ruby's building and upset a tomcat rummaging for breakfast. In the early morning sun the street had a new character, one of lost affluence and now near-poverty. Instead of music, the street sounds were of barking dogs, crying babies, and shouting mothers.

He looked at this scene with anger and dismay, knowing that the night's profits left the Storyville neighborhood and went into the pockets of some far-removed white men, much like Carruthers and his cronies. Robert thought to himself, "The day more black men can own their businesses, hire their neighbors, and support opportunities for an education and advancement, that's the day we'll be free."

As Robert walked away, a wagon pulled into the street that ran perpendicular to the alley. A 10-year-old black boy sat on newspaper piles in the back of the delivery wagon. The papers—*The New Orleans Daily Picayune*—were stacked up all around him. He grabbed one bound stack and tossed it on the sidewalk as the wagon continued down the street. The two major headlines were "Story of the Massacre," which told readers about the massacre of foreigners in China as a result of the Boxer Rebellion, and "More Soldiers for Manila" and the ongoing conflict between the United States and the Philippines.[9]

Chapter 3

Mid-morning, Monday, 16 July 1900, New Orleans

A middle-aged white man, Gerald Billings, held a newspaper, the *New Orleans Daily States*, open in front of him. This paper, while not as large as the *Picayune* or *Times-Democrat*, garnered a loyal following, especially among those readers who continued to trumpet Confederate philosophies. Billings sat in a large room in the newspaper's main offices, the reporters' 'bullpen'. All around, reporters were busy at their typewriters. The man in front of Billings, Thomas O'Malley, a tall, lanky, 31-year-old man with red hair, listened with his back turned as Billings counted out loud with increasing disbelief.

"...twenty-two, twenty-three, twenty-four...twenty-five, twenty-six, twenty-seven! It's a record! The Major used the word 'nigger' twenty-seven times in one editorial!" Billings cried.

O'Malley turned around at the sound of Billings's exclamation. He didn't laugh at the announcement, even though Billings was trying to goad other reporters into marveling at the brazen race baiting of the paper's editor-in-chief.

In his office, Major Henry J. Hearsey, the elderly editor of the *Daily States*, sat behind his desk scowling at a typewritten document he held. As he read, Hearsey tugged at his gray, pointed beard. His office was in one corner of the bullpen, partitioned by glass and wood panels. Hearsey got up from his desk, walked to his office door, and opened it. He stuck his head out the door, and bellowed.

"O'Malley!"

Thomas got up from his desk with apparent nonchalance and proceeded into the editor's office with all eyes on him. Once in Major Hearsey's office, O'Malley remained standing on the visitor's side of the large oak desk while the Major remained seated, holding court in his office.

"Yes, sir?" O'Malley calmly asked.

Major Hearsey held the typed document in his fist and shook it at O'Malley. "What, in the name of Robert E. Lee, is this?" he asked O'Malley.

"My article, sir," O'Malley answered simply.

Major Hearsey's face began to redden. "I know it's your article, O'Malley," Hearsey raged. "What in Sam Hill do you mean by saying, and I quote, 'The victim had little choice but admit to the crime in the face of threats against his life; however, his confession guaranteed his death by lynching at the hands of the mob.'"

The editor put the document down on his desk and leaned toward O'Malley. "Victim?" he screamed. Without waiting for O'Malley to respond, the Major continued, "You imply he was innocent. That nigger was guilty as hell."

O'Malley maintained his calm. "There was no conclusive evidence, sir," O'Malley stated. "And no official trial."

“The woman he ravished identified him!” Hearsey countered with no doubt that he could be wrong.

O’Malley continued with his argument. “She was under pressure from her husband,” he recalled from his research and interviews. “The man she accused claimed he only went to the back door of her house asking for work.”

Major Hearsey looked at his reporter in disbelief. “And when he saw she was alone,” he argued, “he took advantage of her like the beast he was. After all, he confessed.” That scenario seemed to close the case in Hearsey’s mind.

“That’s my point, sir.” O’Malley would not give in to his boss’s illogic. “He confessed under very adverse circumstances, and he was denied a fair trial. That’s supposed to be the foundation of our justice system. Innocent until proven guilty in a court of law.”

Major Hearsey threw the typewritten article down on his desk in exasperation. Most of the individual pages ended up on the floor. “You and your kind are so naive, O’Malley,” Hearsey said. “You know too well that the police and courts have done damn all to protect our women, and that leaves no other recourse but justice by the people.”

Hearsey looked at his reporter for a moment, genuinely believing that no other argument was needed. When O’Malley said nothing and just looked at his boss, Major Hearsey realized that a final point was needed. “That’s why I called you in here, O’Malley.” Hearsey was now speaking from the full authority of his position as well as the privilege of his race and class.“You insinuated in your draft that lynching is wrong, and you know full well what the editorial position of this newspaper is."

O'Malley barely held back his anger. "Yes, sir, but I also know the laws of this nation."

Major Hearsey stood up suddenly, knocking over a glass of iced tea. He pointed his right index finger directly at O'Malley. "See what you've done. Not to mention that I did not bring you on to this paper for legal advice. You're here, O'Malley, because I know a good reporter when I read one."

O'Malley was not expecting this statement and continued to listen to his boss in silence.

Major Hearsey went on. "You can dig out a story better than anyone, but I'm warning you!" The editor clearly enunciated and emphasized each of his next six words.

"Stay…away…from…the…Negro…problem."

Slightly confused, O'Malley asked for clarification. "I'm not sure what you mean?"

Rather than answer with a clear-cut rationale, Hearsey asked O'Malley, "How did you get this story anyway? I thought Lindsey covered the county beat?"

Again, O'Malley felt a bit off balance with the divergent line of questioning. After a moment, he answered, "Lindsey asked me to cover for him yesterday. His wife had a baby boy."

This news completely disrupted the direction the conversation had been heading at the start. "Excellent," Major Hearsey declared with a huge grin. "Another good Confederate soldier!"

"Uh, I beg your pardon, sir?" O'Malley asked, even more confused.

"What? Oh, nothing, O'Malley," Hearsey said, trying to mop up the iced tea with his pocket handkerchief. Giving up the cause, Major Hearsey thought he should go back to why he'd brought O'Malley into his office in the first place. "Just stick to the city's police beat, O'Malley," he ordered. "Any more stories like this one," he said, shaking one of the article's damper pages at his reporter, "and you're out!"

O'Malley stood quietly for just a moment, long enough to internally sigh at the illogic of Major Hearsey's argument. He'd only covered the county police beat because a colleague was indisposed. Similar stories were happening in the city as well. Hearsey had praised him for his solid reporting and writing skills. Handling any potential story with fairness seemed to be what Hearsey valued. Yet, clearly, fairness, justice, and solid First Amendment reporting did not apply to New Orleans' or Louisiana's Negro citizens.

"Yes, sir," was all O'Malley said in response, other than asking, "Is that all?"

"Yes, you can go, O'Malley, but consider yourself warned."

O'Malley left the editor's office and hightailed it back to his desk, where he grabbed his notebook and pen and tucked them into his worn leather attaché case his parents had given him almost a decade ago when he graduated from college. He threw the case's leather strap over his left shoulder and headed toward the bullpen's exit. Billings chased after him, catching up to O'Malley outside the *Daily States* building.

Billings took O'Malley by the elbow and hurriedly led him across the street, dodging traffic, into the press club. Brass railings stretched almost the entire length of the club's main room, which housed the bar, a few tables with chairs, and a sitting area with arm chairs. Several of the city's older reporters sat in this area reading through their competitors' newspapers. Billings guided O'Malley to the bar and motioned to the bartender.

"Two Irish, Peter," Billings ordered.

The bartender filled two shot glasses with Irish whiskey and put them in front of the men. Billings raised his glass and said, "Mother's milk to an Irishman! Cheers, O'Malley!"

Both Billings and O'Malley downed their whiskies in one swallow.

"I'm quitting, Gerald," O'Malley announced to Billings, who didn't take him seriously.

"My dear boy," he chuckled.

With the whiskey giving him a bit of false bravado, O'Malley stated, "I mean it this time."

"You always mean it, Thomas," Billings laughed, "but nothing's changed." Billings motioned Peter for another round, and before O'Malley could stop him, they were both presented with a refreshed shot glass.

"As far as I know," Billings continued, "the *Picayune* and the *Times-Democrat* still don't have openings for full-time reporters. And the *Item* sure doesn't have the money to pay you. Besides, what makes you think they'd take you on anyway?"

O'Malley hurried into his response, eager to share his thoughts. "I know they don't have jobs, but I've come up with a new tactic," downing his second shot as though to bolster much-needed courage for this most recent plan.

Billings, wiping his lips with the back of his left sleeve, chortled. "Short of murdering one of their reporters, I don't have a clue what could get you in their doors."

O'Malley turned to face Billings square on. He picked up his train of thought, expressing it with a serious tone only a journalist could muster. "A feature article that will prove to one or both papers that I'd be an asset to them," he declared, believing this statement to be his true way to success with another newspaper.

Billings asked for clarification. "An article on what?"

Rather than answering his colleague, O'Malley grinned broadly and said, "Top secret, Gerald, but I'll give you a hint."

Billings seemed to show a bit more interest.

O'Malley went on. "What problem does the city seem to be at a complete loss to resolve?"

Without hesitation, Billings answered, "Without a doubt, the sewage problem."

Peter the bartender overheard this last remark and said, "Now, ain't that the truth!"

Ignoring Peter, O'Malley entreated his colleague, "Be serious, Gerald."

Billings thought for a moment, giving O'Malley the impression that he was taking his fellow reporter's plan with full and serious consideration.

"I've got it!" Billings exclaimed. "How to tax the revenue earned by the city's many ladies of the evening!" Billings laughed out loud once again then continued, "No, they wouldn't touch that problem. It would mean the women would have to up their prices, and that would cut into the city fathers' wallets. Not to mention that client names would most likely show up as splashy—and embarrassing—headlines."

When Billings saw that O'Malley found no humor in his ridicule, he turned to his colleague and said with gentle seriousness, "Do tell, Thomas."

"Never mind, Gerald," O'Malley said with a sigh. "You aren't taking me seriously, and I'm not going to waste any more energy or time on you."

Realizing that he really had hurt the feelings of this promising reporter whom he genuinely liked, Billings put both his hands on O'Malley's shoulders and looked him straight in the eyes. "I'm truly sorry, Thomas. Forgive me. I really do want to know what you have in mind." Billings could feel the tension in O'Malley's shoulders ease up a bit so he smiled to his colleague in encouragement. "Come on," he implored Thomas. "Tell me."

After a brief hesitation, O'Malley said with as much confidence as he could muster, "I will only say that it has to do with the 'Negro problem'," holding up both hands and giving air quotes as he said the last two words.

Billings started to chuckle but cut himself off and said, "What, are you going to be the next big muckraker[10]?"

"Maybe I am," Thomas answered. He continued, "I've been looking into what's going on in New Orleans related to how Negros are treated, and I think I've uncovered a possible story with a solution that would please a lot of whites and a number of Negroes as well."

Billings suddenly became quite serious and spoke in true earnest, flavored with a bit of fear, to O'Malley. "You're playing with dynamite, Thomas," Billings warned. "Not only with the Major, but there are a lot of people out there who think the only solution is another war, and I don't mean between North and South."

O'Malley stayed quiet, not sure where Billings was headed.

"I know one or two Yankees who'd gladly join in the battle," Billings said, "especially since this time the war will be against the Negroes."

O'Malley started to totally reject Billings's ludicrous idea when the senior journalist interrupted him and said definitively, "Be very careful, my boy, or you'll find yourself swinging from the nearest tree."

Chapter 4

Morning, Wednesday, 18 July 1900, New Orleans

On this bright summer morning with the hot air barely cooled by an intermittent breeze, Robert worked alongside both black and white men at one of New Orleans' most profitable sawmills.

Wearing heavy cotton overalls with a sleeveless sweat-stained worker's shirt underneath, Robert carried a large plank of wood from a pile over to the saw. Holding the wood steady while other men positioned it to be cut, he then carried the cut wood over to a new pile.

Robert wore thick leather work gloves and heavy-soled boots to protect his hands and feet from the splinters and rough cuts of the wood as it went from log to lumber.

There was a steady rhythm to the work at the sawmill, and all the men—both white and black—seemed to be in sync with one another. A whistle sounded, and the deafening shrill of the saws died away. The men left their posts and gathered in groups with their lunch pails.

Robert took his accustomed place near but not among several other men, both black and white, and quietly ate his lunch alone. The other workmen laughed and joked among themselves. Just as Robert was finishing his lunch, the foreman, a balding middle-aged white man carrying a clipboard, approached the group.

Stepping up to Robert, the foreman stated, "Robert, I'd like to put you on another job for a few days."

Showing a bit of concern, Robert asked, "Has there been something wrong with my work on the cutting team?"

"Not at all," the foreman was quick to answer. "I just need a man with your strength to help with the unloading. Tompkins took sick and won't be back for a few days. You can go back to the cutting team when he returns."

Robert stood up and tucked his waste paper in his lunch pail. He spoke directly to his boss. "Yes, sir. Who do I report to?"

The foreman paused for a moment, scratching at the sunburned and peeling skin on his scalp. He appeared to be thinking how to answer Robert's question. "Tompkins was the team supervisor, but I can't put you in that position since you'll be new to the team." The foreman looked up confidently at Robert with his answer. "Report directly to me if there're any problems. You'll be working with Tompkins's partner, a young punk name of Mickey."

Robert shuffled from one foot to the other upon hearing his new partner's name. Reputations traveled fast through the sawmill, and no one had much good to say about this Mickey character.

As if to put Robert at ease, the foreman said with a placating tone, "My best advice with Mickey is just do your work and ignore him the best you can."

Robert did not say anything.

In an attempt to bring a bit of lightness back to the moment, the foreman said, "I'm convinced his mama dropped him on his head when he was a baby."

The other workmen laughed but not Robert, although he did give a slight nod of acknowledgement to his boss.

He could always count on fair treatment from this foreman, and Robert knew he'd continue to do well at the sawmill as long as he kept up the quality of his work, worked steadily, and treated his coworkers and bosses with the same respect he expected. So far Robert was square on all counts. Gathering up his lunch pail and gloves, Robert followed the foreman to the unloading area, feeling confident that this temporary shift in assignment would ingratiate him further with his supervisor.

Pine logs denuded of branches were lined up in rows and stacked atop wagons, each with a team of four men—two unloaders on top of the wagon's stack of wood and two receivers at the wagon's base ready to take the logs handed down to them. From there, the receivers passed them on to a second team that carried the logs from the wagon to the cutting area.

The foreman pointed to a young white man in his late teens, Mickey, who was standing on top of the logs in the first wagon to Robert's left. One other unloader, a nondescript middle-aged white man, shared the job. There was only one receiver at the base of the wagon, a white man who looked older than his forty-five years. Weather, hard work, and going hungry some days along with tobacco and alcohol every day had worn this man down to his core—chest sunken, shoulders stooped, and hardly enough meat on his bones to keep him standing. No wonder the foreman wanted a man of Robert's strength and endurance on this particular work team Robert thought to himself.

The foreman shouted up to Mickey, "Hey, Mickey. I've got you a new partner for a few days. Name's Robert, Robert Charles."

Robert looked up at Mickey and nodded his head in greeting, shouting up, "Nice to meet you, Mickey."

Mickey, ignoring Robert, asked the foreman directly, "Why'd ya bring me a buck?"

Robert clenched his jaws but knew it was best to let the foreman handle this situation.

The foreman, not hiding his disgust, responded, "Now, I'll have none of that, Mickey. I brought you someone who'll make you look good. Maybe with him around you'll stop slacking off, and I'll get my money's worth out of ya."

Robert knew at once that this highly ill-advised comment meant serious trouble. It was clear to Robert that Mickey was not part of New Orleans' *nouveau riche*. Rather, he imagined this angry young man came from a rural area in Louisiana where his family's poverty gave him a rough start to life. It was this insecurity and anger that justified in Mickey's mind the necessity of putting down members of what he believed to be an inferior race. At least that's how Robert saw it. Either that, or Mickey was an out-and-out, mean-hearted Ku Kluxer in the making.

As if to prove Robert's supposition correct, Mickey hawked and spat on the ground in response to the foreman's jibing.

The foreman shook his head, turned to Robert and said, “Remember my advice and you’ll do fine. I don’t want any trouble.”

“Neither do I, sir,” Robert responded as the foreman nodded at him before he turned his back on the wagon and walked away.

Robert remained standing at the base of the wagon for just a moment, but it was long enough for Mickey to say impatiently, “Well, come on, Sambo.”

Robert carried his lunch pail over to the work area’s holding station and returned to his position, all the while trying to rein in his outrage. “The name’s Robert or Charles. Either will do,” he said to Mickey matter of factly.

Mickey turned to the other worker atop the timber wagon and said, “You hear that?” His coworker didn’t reply or react in any way. He just wanted to get the day’s work done and go home in peace. Mickey continued, mocking Robert, “‘Either will do.’” Looking down at Robert, he said again, “Get to it, Sambo.”

Mickey roughly unloaded a log onto Robert’s shoulder. Robert managed to balance the log while the next team of two men took it from him and carried it to the storage area. Robert had unloaded two logs when Mickey decided to make Robert look bad. Pretending to lose his grip, Mickey dropped the next log onto Robert’s shoulder. Robert’s knees buckled under the sudden and unexpected weight of the log, but he managed to move out of the way before both he and the log fell to the ground. As it fell, the log grazed a bare area of Robert’s shoulder and took off a swatch of skin, leaving a raw, bloody patch.

"You clumsy mule," Mickey spat out at Robert. "My grandma, she's stronger'n you any ol' time."

Robert tilted his head back to stare at Mickey with rage in his eyes. He took a step toward the wagon, grabbing hold of a log to pull himself up to the top. Mickey took a sudden step backwards, stumbled, and fell on his butt. With the tension broken by the startled look on Mickey's face, the other workmen laughed. Robert turned and walked away, knowing he was on the dangerous end of this outcome.

As a woman in the main office tended to Robert's wound, the foreman handed Robert his pay envelope, telling him, "Take the rest of the day off, Robert." He paused. "No, you'd better take the next few days off. Give Mickey a chance to cool down. I hate being two men short, but we'll manage. I'll have you back on the cutting team next week."

Robert thumbed through the money in the envelope, counting it, then looked up at the foreman inquisitively.

"I had to dock you a half day of pay for today," the foreman explained to Robert. "And I can't pay you for the rest of the days you'll take off until you're strong enough to go back to work."

Robert did his best to keep a lid on his fury. He was paying for some other person's behavior. Rather than letting loose his rage at the injustice, Robert stated firmly, “I’d rather keep working. I’m okay for the cutting team, and I need the money.”

Shaking his head, the foreman stated with finality, “I’m sorry, Robert, really, but that’s a mighty nasty scrape. And like I said, there’s liable to be more trouble. Mickey is telling everyone that you talked back to him then threatened him.”

This falsehood raised Robert’s ire enough that he let his voice go up an octave. “I never said a word to that punk. I walked away without a word!”

“I know you did,” the foreman said, “but you know what happens when rumors get started ’round here.” The foreman paused and laughed, ignoring the seriousness with which Robert considered this unfair treatment. “You remember last month when the story about Horace’s mule started spreading?” the foreman asked Robert. “By the end of the day half the mill believed that the brute had killed and eaten two old ladies.”

Not amused, Robert merely responded, “Yes, sir.” As he stood up to go, his shoulder and demeanor bandaged up tight, Robert said in monotone, “I’ll be in as usual on Monday morning.”

Believing that he had dealt with this situation in all fairness and with the proper solution, the foreman said, “It’s for the best, Robert.”

Had the foreman ended his statement with that phrase, Robert could’ve walked away and been back to better spirits by the end of the day. But the foreman added, “And you realize, don’t you, Robert, that it’s nothing personal. I got nothing against you. You’re a good worker. I just don’t want any trouble.”

Robert folded his pay envelope and stuck it in his pocket. Everything that happened today was very personal. Robert had been disrespected by some lowlife kid in front of his coworkers. He'd been docked nearly a week's pay, money he very much needed for rent, food, and his dream of getting out of this racist nation where a man was treated like a dog by other men. It was reminding himself of this dream that brought Robert 'round so that his final words to the foreman were a simple, "Yes, sir."

A jumbled mix of rage and hurt with a hint of shame at his acquiescence boiled beneath the surface as Robert left the sawmill. He felt the intensity of a frenzied mess of feelings, passions, and impulses without fully understanding them all at this moment. But he knew he would not let them go until he did better appreciate their meaning and place.

Chapter 5

Afternoon, Wednesday, 18 July 1900, New Orleans

Major Hearsey stormed into the *Daily States*' bullpen waving a copy of a rival newspaper. He approached the middle of the room, stopped, and began to read out loud to the group of reporters.

"'...and to conclude,'" Hearsey began. He continued with much animation, reading, "'...should it be necessary to protect the voting rights of our colored citizens, the state militia should be ready to take arms against those who defy the Constitution. Either we protect the rights of Negroes through the proper channels, or we should call on these citizens to protect themselves with whatever means necessary.' Have you ever heard of such insane rot?" the Major cried.

Billings expressed disbelief at what he'd just heard. "Did the *Picayune* write that?" he asked.

"No, it was a speech by some Yankee rabble-rouser," Major Hearsey clarified. "But the *Picayune* reprinted it word for word. Thank Robert E. Lee the paper's editors had the sense to denounce this treason. Of course, their reply was hardly strong enough."

The Major turned to Lowery and Billings, "I want you, Lowery, along with Billings, to start working on reports discrediting this Yankee. Parker, you work on an editorial explaining why disenfranchisement is necessary. I'll be in my office writing a proper condemnation. And O'Malley..." The Major hesitated before continuing.

O'Malley looked up from his desk where his fingers were poised over his typewriter's keyboard. "Yes, sir?" O'Malley asked.

Major Hearsey put his fists on his hips and turned to face O'Malley. "Don't you dare touch this story, O'Malley," the Major ordered.

After leaving the sawmill, covered in dust and dirt despite only a half-day at work, Robert entered a bath house along the busy New Orleans' street. He carried a beat-up leather satchel with him that held his fresh clothes. About forty minutes later he emerged clean and dressed in a stylish brown suit. Robert walked down the street and entered the post office a few blocks down.

Standing at the island placed in the center of the post office, Robert took an envelope out of his inner lapel pocket and put it on the island top. Taking out a pen, Robert addressed the envelope to the International Migration Society, Passage to Liberia Fund. Once fully addressed and stamped, Robert got ready to drop the letter in the mail slot. He hesitated.

"Yes," he thought, "I must keep an eye on the prize."

Robert secretly wished his letter safe passage and dropped it in the slot. Robert collected his mail from a post office box, putting the unopened mail in his right coat pocket. Robert held onto a newspaper published by the Migration Society, gripping it tightly as he left the post office.

That errand completed, Robert headed toward the clothing store he frequented on Poydras Street. When Robert entered the store, Hyman Levy, a salesman, approached. He was a man of medium height and with an olive complexion. His dark hair was peppered with gray. He appeared to be about 50 years old and wore wire-rimmed glasses.

"Curtis!" Hyman declared enthusiastically. "It's been a while and it's good to see you again. Tell me, how have you been?"

Smiling at the older man and shaking Hyman's outstretched hand, Robert said, "I'm doing all right, Mr. Levy. How are you? Is your daughter feeling any better?"

Hyman replied with concern. "We've been to three doctors," he said. "You'd think that one of them could tell us something. All they ever say is that she has a 'delicate nature', which is crazy. She was a rambunctious child, a real tomboy. I just don't understand her weakness now. My wife thinks we should take her to New York, to see a specialist."

"That sounds like a good idea to me," Robert commented, pausing a moment before speaking again. "I've read about a relatively new hospital that's opened up in Baltimore," he said. "Johns Hopkins. They're supposed to have the latest and best, especially since their School of Medicine is up and running as well. Maybe one of their doctors could tell you something definite. I hope so anyway, and Baltimore's closer than New York."

"That's kind of you, Curtis," Hyman responded, "but don't let me waste your time with my troubles. What can I do for you today?"

Smiling, Robert said, "It's never a waste of time when we talk. I always enjoy it. But since you ask, I'd like to buy a new suit. Something lighter weight for summer. Looks like it's going to be a hot one."

Levy smiled and nodded in agreement.

"Could you show me what you have in blue?"" Robert asked.

"Certainly," Hyman answered, turning away from Robert. "Come over here and look at these." He led Robert to the back corner of the shop. Hyman sorted through a number of men's suits on the rack and pulled out three lighter-weight ones, laying them out on a nearby table. "Here are three different styles," he said. "And feel the material. Soft and lightweight."

Robert immediately was attracted to the suit in the center, picking it up and holding it in front of himself. It was a navy-blue pinstripe suit with a matching vest. There was something about this particular outfit that spoke to Robert. He could see himself striding through New Orleans' nightlife in this fine-looking suit.

"I'd like to try this one," he said.

"Excellent choice!" Hyman declared. "You go on into the changing area, and I'll be back with you in a moment to measure for the alterations."

After his fitting and putting a down payment of five dollars on the suit, Robert walked to his favorite restaurant, Plantain's Porch. He entered the busy establishment, a small homey place filled with an all-black clientele. A short, heavy-set black woman, Ma Plantain, greeted Robert as he entered.

"Look at you, boy!" Ma declared in her high-pitched voice with a very Southern accent. "You so skinny. I'd swear you haven't eaten none since you was here last."

Robert laughed and smiled down on Ma Plantain. "You think anyone smaller than Pa is skinny. I'll admit, though, I haven't tasted anything decent since you fed me last."

Beaming, Ma guided Robert to a table by the wall, talking all the way. "Of course you ain't," she said to Robert with an indoor voice and a grin. The next second Ma shouted in a surprisingly deeper voice, "Pa, get yourself out here and say 'Hi' to Robert. Sally, child, hustle to it and bring this thirsty man a beer. No doubt his mouth be drier than an oak tree in the desert!"

Sally, the Plantain's daughter, was a pretty girl of seventeen. She ran out of the kitchen to the back of the restaurant. She returned holding a cold bottle of beer and a glass. She smiled shyly at Robert, putting the beer and glass in front of him. She began to open the bottle, but her mother took it from her.

"I'll do that, sweetie," she said to Sally. "You run on into the kitchen and tell your daddy to get his self out here."

"Yes, Ma," Sally obeyed, running off to the kitchen.

Robert sat down at his table, smiling up at Ma. "She gets prettier every day," Robert said.

Ma looked over her shoulder and then back to Robert. "She be gettin' too pretty," Ma worried. "Pa liked to kill a customer the other day over that child."

Knowing he wouldn't get his meal until he heard the story, Robert politely asked, "What'd he do?"

"Some low life come in here and mistook our baby for some trashy kind of girl," Ma obliged. "Asked her what's for dessert, and he wasn't referring to my pee-can pie."

Robert laughed out loud, throwing his head back. At that moment, a large middle-aged black man weighing around three-hundred pounds approached the table.

Pa Plantain looked down at Robert and greeted his diner. "Hey, Buster," Pa said.

"How're you doing, Pa?" Robert responded in kind. Robert stood, and the two men shook hands while Pa wiped his left hand on the large apron he wore.

"Can't complain," Pa said. "You lookin' good. Yourself?"

"I'm feeling all right," Robert reassured him. Sitting back at his table, Robert asked, "What did you cook up tonight?"

"The sweetest, hottest, tastiest shrimp jambalaya you ever done taste," Pa declared. "And honey-baked cornbread," he quickly added.

Robert looked up at Pa and smacked his lips. "Umm um!" Robert said. "Now, stop talking and bring me a bowl," he directed Pa. He paused a moment before adding, "Make it two. I'm expecting a friend any minute."

“Sure ’nough,” Pa said. “Sally’ll bring it out to you. By the way, put me down for two more issues of the *Voice*. Take the subscription out of the cost of dinner.”

Robert took his small notebook and fountain pen out of his left breast pocket and marked down Pa’s subscription. “Consider it done,” he said. “And take care of yourself, Pa.”

Pa rested his left hand on Robert’s shoulder and said with sincerity, “You too, Buster. Stay outta trouble.”

Robert smiled up at Pa and said, “That’s my plan.”

Pa went back to the kitchen. Left alone at his table, Robert took the mail out of his right-side coat pocket and opened a letter postmarked from Mississippi. The letter he read seemed to bother him. He did not see Lenard Pierce enter the restaurant.

Lenard, a small 19-year-old man with skin darker than Robert’s, sat down across from the bigger man and waited for his friend to look up. While he waited, Lenard picked up the newspaper and tried to read an article on the front page.

He proceeded softly, slowly, and quietly out loud with great difficulty. “The ex…ex-puh…something…led by Re…Rev…Reverend…somebody…to Li…bear…ia tree…three months a-go has bean called a f…fa…”

Robert put his letter down and took the newspaper from his young friend’s hands. He said, “What did you read, Lenard?”

“I don’t know,” Lenard answered. “That top bit. About Africa, I think. What does it say?”

Robert read out loud.

"'The expedition led by Reverend Samuel Beale to Liberia three months ago has been called a failure. A recent letter from a member of the expedition party to this newspaper reveals that one child has died from fever and only a few weeks of provisions remain. The author of the letter requests funds from the Society and donations from concerned citizens to assist the group on returning to America.'"

Robert put the newspaper down harshly on the table.

Lenard didn't respond to this angry jester. Instead he stated with a shake of his head, "Man, I wish I could read like you."

Robert ignored what his friend just said. "It shouldn't have failed," Robert stated vehemently. "Not if they were prepared for any eventuality. I could understand it if they had harsh weather once they arrived in Africa, but all reports have said the conditions are good right now."

Not sure how to respond, Lenard said, "Maybe they just want to come home."

"No," Robert said vehemently. "You don't walk away from your friends and family and leave behind most of what little you own without being sure you want to go. Everyone who has committed themselves to going over knows there will be hardships." Robert paused then continued with more enthusiasm. "But whatever comes out of the struggle will belong to us," he said, nodding around at the almost-full restaurant. "The corn we grow will be ours, not 'one for the Master, one for the Dame'. The only sharing we'll have to do is with each other…giving ourselves a helping hand."

Lenard asked eagerly, “So what went wrong?”

“I don’t know,” Robert admitted. “My guess would be that most of their seed rotted on the voyage over. Before the next expedition we have to find a better way to keep provisions and supplies from going bad.”

“How do we do that?” Lenard asked.

“We teach ourselves,” Robert answered. He thought for a moment and said with enthusiasm. “I just read about some interesting agricultural research coming out of the Tuskegee Institute. They’ve got a new head of the Agricultural Department. I think his name’s Washington.”

“Like the president?” Lenard asked.

Robert smiled at his young friend. “Probably named for George,” Robert laughed. “But I may be wrong about his name. The president of Tuskegee is Booker T. Washington. That may have been who I was thinking about, but I do know they have a really interesting new man studying about farming. I heard he was born a slave.”

Lenard gave Robert a look of disbelief then asked his friend, “When will you be going to Africa?”

Robert gave Lenard a serious but hopeful look. “I’m saving every penny I can right now. I do want to know that more of the problems are worked out first.”

“Whaddya mean?” Lenard asked.

“Anytime there’re children in the group,” Robert said, “their safety comes first. We can’t have children, or anybody else for that matter, but especially children, dying on the voyage over or right after settling in Africa.”

"How can we be sure that don't happen?" Lenard asked.

"We have to make sure that every group has people in it with the right skills," he answered Lenard. Robert continued, "There has to be one doctor—at least—as well as a blacksmith, carpenter, teacher, and others. And despite his good intentions, Reverend Beale was the wrong man to lead the group. Faith is okay up to a point, but you need someone who knows how to survive here on Earth, not just make sure our souls get to heaven. We need someone who knows how to tell people what to do…to take charge even if it means making people mad sometimes. You can shout all you want to heaven, but making yourself heard here on Earth is what counts."

Lenard smiled broadly and said, "You'd be good."

"At making people mad?" Robert asked with a grin.

Both men laughed as Sally brought out two steaming bowls of jambalaya and a plate piled with cornbread. Robert took his napkin out from under his fork and unfolded it on his lap. He said to Sally, "You're an angel, Sally. Do you know my friend, Lenard Pierce?"

Sally answered shyly. "No, we haven't met."

Robert looked back at Lenard. "Les, this is the Plantain's daughter, Sally." Robert turned to look back at Sally. "Sally, this is Lenard, who also goes by Les," Robert said, completing the introductions. "The two of you are about the same age. Les, you're nineteen, right? And Sally will soon be eighteen."

Lenard looked up at Sally and said quickly, "Pleased to meet ya, Sally."

Giving Lenard a slight smile and looking down to the floor, Sally reverted to what she knew best, serving people.

"Can I bring you a beer, Mr. Pierce?" she asked.

Genuinely surprised, Lenard said, "Mister? Ain't no one ever called me Mister Pierce before. Beer sounds good, Miss Plantain."

Sally giggled, turned, and went to the back of the restaurant for the beer. Lenard followed her with his eyes, smiling slightly.

Robert, in good humor again, mocked Lenard. "Best keep your eyes in their sockets, Lenard," he warned. "Last man who looked at the Plantains' daughter that way left here with his head shaped like a frying pan."

"She sure is pretty," was Lenard's only response.

Robert picked up his soup spoon and said, "Eat up, my boy. We have to be at the Bay Street Club in an hour."

Inside Stendel's Drugstore, Thomas O'Malley sat at the dining counter eating apple pie and drinking coffee. Two New Orleans policemen, Mora and Cantrelle, entered the drugstore and sat down next to O'Malley.

O'Malley greeted the men with familiarity, "Anything happening worth writing about, fellas?

Cantrelle responded, "Mora here got his foot stuck in Madame Claude's door."

Quick to answer this insult, Mora said, “That’s ’cause her workin’ girls got a look at your ugly mug and slammed the door on us.”

O’Malley laughed. “Was it a ‘friendly’ call, or were you there on business?”

Mora answered, “We got a tip that customers were having cash lifted while they were…uh…indisposed.”

O’Malley said, “Don’t suppose you could point me in the direction of a customer or two for some interviews?”

Cantrelle answered in disbelief, “And have their wives read about it in the afternoon edition and find out how hubby spends his lunch hour? Not hardly.”

“Well,” O’Malley said, “if you haven’t got anything for me I guess I’ll be heading out.”

Cantrelle wasn’t ready to stop. He mocked, “You could go interview one of the girls.”

Cantrelle and Mora laughed. O’Malley stood up from his stool and smiled slightly, “Take it easy, fellas.”

“See you around, O’Malley,” the two officers responded in unison.

With no story prospects, O’Malley left the drugstore.

Chapter 6

Evening, Wednesday, 18 July 1900, New Orleans

Early evening saw the streets slowing down and the number of stars in the sky brightening by the thousands. Robert had noticed, however, that with more street lamps and light from nearly every store and apartment along the way, it was getting harder to see distinct stars and constellations.

Robert sure missed living out in the country where he could lie flat on his back in an empty field and gaze up for hours at these glittering little miracles. Now that was the epitome of free will! He especially liked picking out constellations' designs. He knew most of their official names, but Robert loved to follow a trail of stars, see his own design in them, and use his imagination to come up with a special name for the constellation of his making. Copiah Catalina was his latest creation, named for his nearly nine-year-old niece back in Mississippi. Robert imagined the stars to be shaped like the sleek wild panthers that called out at night in the wilds of his home county of Copiah, a name that meant "Calling Panther" in the native language of the Choctaws from the Bayou Pierre region of Mississippi.[11]

Robert and Lenard arrived at the Union Sons' Hall Bay Street Club, a black social club. They paused outside the entrance, a modest double doorway without windows on either side. They read the placard posted on the wall. The announcement told them about the evening's events, a discussion of voting rights and migration to Africa followed by dancing, only the words 'voting rights' had been crossed out on the printed sign. Refreshments would be served. Robert paused for a moment as he looked at the edited sign, wondering why the change in the evening's program. No doubt somebody had put some pressure on the club's manager, Robert thought to himself. He tried to set aside this thought as the two men entered the club.

Robert and Lenard stepped into a large room with a podium at one end and rows of chairs facing it. There was an aisle down the center of the chairs. About two-thirds of the chairs were full with both men and women, ranging in skin tone from a light café latte to dark chocolate and of all different ages.

The two men found seats on the third row near the center aisle, with Robert sitting next to the aisle. He scanned the audience and was surprised to see Virginia Banks across from him. An attractive woman in her mid-twenties, Virginia had been Robert's on-again, off-again girlfriend for the past three years. He was surprised to see her here tonight, since they hadn't been out together in quite a few months.

Virginia was dressed in a simple off-white dress with pale blue ribbons. Her long brown hair was twisted onto the back of her head and held in place with a French comb. She watched Robert as he sat down, and when he caught her eye Virginia gave Robert a slight smile and a nod.

Thomas O'Malley returned to the *Daily States'* building and entered the empty and darkened bullpen. He went to his desk and turned on a lamp. He unlocked the bottom drawer and removed a stack of publications written by black authors about the 'Negro problem'. He put the articles on his desk and sorted through them, occasionally pausing to read one more closely.

One that caught his attention was an article from a couple of years earlier in 1898, telling how journalist Ida B. Wells had brought her anti-lynching campaign to the White House. She called for President William McKinley to use his leadership to bring about reforms that would put an end to this most horrible and violent of crimes against the American Negro. Thomas had been reading Wells's articles for nearly a decade and admired her courage in writing boldly about lynching in the South. She did not hesitate to describe in detail the inhuman torture and suffering white mobs inflicted on their black victims, putting her own life at risk to expose these crimes.

Thomas knew she applied the highest of journalistic ethics to everything she wrote, something he prided in his own reporting. However, Thomas hoped he could demonstrate just a hint of her courage in his plan to write an article about how New Orleans was approaching the growing tensions between whites and their Negro neighbors. He just did not yet feel connected to the story. Yes, he believed that what was happening to Negroes in

America was unconscionable, but here he was, a white man originally from North Carolina. Had he made enough effort to learn about and listen to this so-called problem from a black man's point of view? Thomas knew the answer and was resolved to do something to change it.

A portly middle-aged gentleman stood at the podium speaking to the audience at the Union Sons' Hall. Robert listened intently, but Lenard fidgeted in his seat.

With both hands on the podium, the speaker continued. "…and finally, I would like to say that Liberia offers us something we have never had in this country—the freedom to govern ourselves without the fear that these rights will be taken away."

As the speech ended, the audience applauded politely, but not enthusiastically. Several people raised their hands to ask questions, and the speaker pointed to an older black man, who stood.

After clearing his throat, the man spoke, saying, "I'm an American. Why should I have to go clear over to Africa for the right to vote? I've worked this land since I was eight years old. Granted, I wasn't born free, but I am free now! This is my country too. It's not just the white man's. I'll admit it hasn't been so easy living here at times, but it's home."

The speaker directed his answer to the older man, who had returned to his seat. "We can make a home for ourselves in Liberia. As long as we have family and friends with us, we have home. We'll make the soil ours, and the fruits of our labors will belong to us."

A young man stood up from the back of the audience and interrupted the speaker. "We have to stay here and fight," the young man argued. "Running away to Africa will only give the white man what he wants. It's just like giving in to them."

Another man, middle-aged, turned around from a few rows forward to address the young man, who was still standing. "Isn't that what we're doing now?" the man asked. He continued with growing vehemence. "I haven't voted in two years, since they passed the grandfather clause. And I go to sleep every night worrying about my sons...wondering how they're doing back in Mississippi. Wondering if they accidentally bumped into some white woman and got strung up for it. They've got us running scared. I say that we're already running away. We might as well be running to someplace where we feel safe."

Sitting at his desk in the bullpen, O'Malley sorted through an abundance of research material looking for a particular article. When he found it, O'Malley began reading an article about a lynching. Clearly disturbed by what he read, O'Malley put the article down and picked up a brochure advertising "Passage to Liberia." He sorted through the pile of papers and pulled together all the literature on the back-to-Africa movement.

As the debate about going back to Africa continued, Robert stood to make a statement. He stepped into the aisle and faced the audience, slowly walking backwards while talking to the group. When he took his stance in front of the podium, he spoke softly, but soon his words were filled with an increasing dynamism that mesmerized his audience.

"If I could just say a few words. Everything that's been said tonight is true. We were born here, not Africa. We're no more Africans than the white men are Europeans or British. There should be a place for us here, but, like the gentleman said…" Robert said, pausing as he nodded toward the middle-aged man who had spoken earlier. He continued, "…whites have us running scared. The way I see it, though, we still have some choices left, but each person here better weigh the consequences very carefully. There's no way that all the Negroes in the United States are going to pack up and move to Liberia or other foreign lands, despite what some whites say. But I can say that it is one choice open to us."

He continued, "Some of you have built a life for yourselves here, and you don't want to give it up, especially saying goodbye to family. But you have to know that deciding to stay means keeping your eyes to the ground, not looking the 'boss man' in the face, or asking for more than he's willing to give. Others of you, like the young man in the back, will choose to fight. We all know the consequences of that. Don't misunderstand me. A man has the right to stand up and defend himself or his family, but it has to be done with eyes open wide, knowing the cost...and we all know that cost could be the highest any man is asked to pay."

Murmurs of agreement came from the listeners.

"Look at going to Africa as a chance to redirect all that anger into living instead of dying," Robert said with an added shot of enthusiasm. "Why fight when you can't win? Why not look at Liberia, the land of true liberty, as an opportunity with limitless possibilities? I see a world over there where we can work hard all day on land that we own then go home at night to our families and know that our children are safe...knowing that they'll grow up proud of you and themselves."

While Robert spoke, the audience sat spellbound by his words and voice. Virginia couldn't take her eyes off of him. Lenard sat in awe of his friend, and Lewis Forstall sat quietly at the back of the audience watching and listening intently to Robert.

"It's important to each of us as human beings to feel respect from our fellow men...and women...but each of us knows from personal experience that our nation is taking a bad turn down an evil path. When newspapers in our very own city of New Orleans are calling Negroes 'beasts', 'animals', 'savages', and 'brutes', how can we ever get a fair shake? Our fellow white citizens read about us as less than human, and for the ones who already are predisposed to thinking of us as inferior......well, I don't have to say it again. These are dangerous times. But I choose to see them as hopeful times as well. We can continue to learn. We must continue to demand and defend our rights under the Constitution. Most important, we must continue to believe in ourselves and the possibilities open to us."

As Robert paused, a man from the audience asked out loud, "Are you willing to stand tall here on this land if necessary?"

Robert didn't hesitate to answer, standing taller as he spoke, "I stand tall every day, knowing when I can assert myself and when I must give the expected answer. Neither way changes my worth. I am the man I want to be, and I will be responsible for myself and my choices. Right now I choose to look freedom in the eyes and keep my sights set on Africa."

In the quiet seconds after he finished speaking, Robert stepped away from the podium to return to his seat, but the moment was accented by a few hands clapping in appreciation for what Robert said. Slowly others joined in until the room reverberated with vigorous applause. Men rushed up to shake Robert's hand and slap him on the back, leaving Robert somewhat overwhelmed by this attention.

As the applause quieted, Robert noticed Virginia was staring at him with a slightly puzzled look on her face. He smiled at her, and she looked away. People began to clear away the chairs to make a dance floor, and Robert worked his way toward Virginia, who was now arranging food on the buffet table. A few band members unpacked their instruments and warmed up to play dance tunes.

A black three-year-old boy ran up to the musicians and pestered the clarinet player, who stopped playing for a moment and spoke to the trombone player, perturbed, "Hey, Bechet. Get your nephew out from under my feet. I can't play with him bugging me."

Bechet, the trombone player, called to the child, "Hey, Sidney Joseph, come on over here and leave Hopkins alone." He then spoke more lovingly to his young nephew. "You can sit on the floor by me, Sid."

The toddler ran over to his uncle and sat next to him on the floor, rocking in time to the music.

O'Malley put a clean sheet of paper into his typewriter to start tapping out a story on the back-to-Africa movement. After about twenty minutes, O'Malley scowled at the page he just typed. He ripped it out of the typewriter, balled it up, and tossed it into the trash can. He gathered up the newspapers and pamphlets he'd been reading as well as the few pages he'd typed, and made them into a parcel. Thomas turned out the lamp and left, carrying the parcel with him.

While a few couples danced to the jazzy beat of the music, Virginia walked around to the front of the buffet table to meet Robert as he handed her a glass of punch. She looked directly at him. "You seem surprised to see me here," Virginia said.

"You're the one who seemed surprised," Robert countered. "I don't know why. I've been interested in migrating to Africa since we met."

"Of course you have," Virginia said. "That's not what surprises me."

Robert gave this young woman a more puzzled look.

"I've just never heard you speak so publicly…or passionately," Virginia observed. "You've always been one to stay out of the limelight…not wanting to bring attention to yourself."

Robert chuckled, taking a sip of punch. "That's definitely true," he said, "but something moved me tonight to have a say." Robert gave Virginia a wink and a small smile. "Maybe seeing you here tonight made me want to impress you."

Virginia didn't respond.

"Did I?" Robert asked.

"Did you what?" Virginia countered, knowing full well what Robert was asking.

"Impress you," Robert answered.

"Why, Mr. Charles," Virginia said with a hint of mocking to her voice, "you spoke with such fervor about Africa and leaving this land that seems so dangerous…I was just plain scared."

"There's nothing fragile about you, Miss Banks," Robert observed drily. "And you certainly don't scare easily."

Virginia laughed, "I guess you do know me." She paused and then said, looking directly at Robert, "But I'll admit that you continue to puzzle me. You have ever since we met for the first time at this club. You would think after nearly three years, I'd know everything about you, but I guess one of the things I like about you, Mr. Robert Charles, is that there seems to always be something more to you."

Robert motioned to some chairs at the side of the room and suggested, "Let's move over here, and maybe I can put a few more pieces of the puzzle together for you."

They moved to the side of the room and sat. There were few people around them.

"Your speech," Virginia said, pausing for a moment. "It was very moving."

"Is that a good thing?" Robert asked.

Virginia didn't answer him directly. Instead, she spoke to her own feelings. "I have no doubt that before too long you'll be on your way to Africa. You dream big, and I've always liked that. I guess I'm ready for something more in my life as well."

"Oh?" Robert queried with an unspoken question.

"I've been serving whites in their homes for nearly ten years now," Virginia continued. "Not to say that I haven't done well for myself."

"In what respect?" Robert asked.

"I've had good people to work for who have treated me decently, at least in comparison to how I'm treated sometimes as a Negro woman in shops and out on the street."

"We deserve more than 'decent' treatment," Robert commented.

"Let's not start down that path, Robert," Virginia cut in. "I want to do something more with my life. Have I seen you since I started sharing a room with Ernestine Goldstein?" she asked.

"Last time we got together, you and she were just moving in together," Robert remembered. "I think you told me she had a job cleaning at Charity Hospital."

"That's right," Virginia smiled. "And working there has sparked her interest in nursing."

"What do you mean?" Robert asked.

Virginia sat forward on her chair and continued with more enthusiasm. "I don't know if you remember about six years ago the New Orleans chapter of the Phyllis Wheatley Club opened the Wheatley Sanitarium and a nursing program so Negro doctors and nurses could have a place to practice medicine. It closed down the next year, but three years ago the New Orleans Medical College took it over, including the nursing school. They have a two-year nursing program for Negro women that offers full-time students free tuition and board in return for working as nurses at their hospital."

"Don't tell me you're thinking about nursing school," Robert said, a bit surprised.

"And why shouldn't I?" Virginia snapped back. "I may have to borrow some of your textbooks to brush up on some subjects, but I can do as well as…"

Robert's laugh cut Virginia off before she could finish her thought. "I knew your spark was under there somewhere," he said. "Of course you can do anything you set your mind to," Robert declared.

They looked at each other for a moment and laughed.

The band began to play a slow dance number that featured the alto saxophone. Robert stood and held his left hand out to Virginia.

"Well, Miss Virginia Banks," Robert said. "Would you honor me with this dance?"

Virginia stood and placed her right hand in Robert's left and smiled into his eyes with acceptance. They walked side-by-side on to the dance floor. Although others were dancing, a path seemed to open up for them as they glided into the center. Their movements were slow and graceful, in perfect complement with each other and the music. Robert pulled Virginia a little closer, and she assented.

Thomas O'Malley, carrying the parcel he'd put together in the newsroom, entered his one-room apartment. He looked around the dingy room, poured himself a drink, and opened a window to let in some fresh air. The faint sounds of music drifted into the room, and Thomas stood alone looking down at the couple who walked along the street laughing. He went back to his desk, sat, and unwrapped the parcel, picking out a copy of *Voice of Missions*. He began to read.

Robert and Virginia walked through the quiet streets holding hands. They reached Virginia's house and mounted the steps. "Would you like to come in for some coffee, Robert?" Virginia asked.

"Sure," Robert answered. "If Ernestine doesn't mind."

"Ernestine is out tonight and won't be back for a while," Virginia said.

Robert, wanting to keep the moment relaxed, said, "I can only stay a little while, anyway. I have to be up early tomorrow."

Virginia took a key out of her clutch purse and unlocked the front door. Robert and Virginia entered the hallway, and Virginia opened a door to their left. Virginia's sitting room was quite warm, and Robert removed his suit jacket. The blood from his injured shoulder had soaked through to his shirt. Virginia gasped at the sight.

"What happened?" she asked. "Were you in a fight?"

Robert looked down at his shoulder. "No," he answered. "I got this trying to avoid a fight. A log dropped on my shoulder this morning at Pelican Sawmill, where I'm working now."

Virginia walked over to Robert and took him by the hand. She led him into the kitchenette and sat Robert down in a straight-backed chair. "Take off your shirt," she directed Robert, taking charge of the situation. "I'll clean the wound and put a fresh bandage on it."

As Robert unbuttoned his shirt, he asked with a hint of a smile, "Already starting to practice at nursing?"

"As a matter of fact, I am," Virginia responded. And with more authority, she demanded, "Now, take off your shirt and sit down."

Robert removed his shirt while Virginia walked to the stove top, picked up the kettle, and poured water into a basin on the counter. She carried the basin over to the table where Robert was sitting. Virginia gently unwrapped the blood-soaked bandage from Robert's shoulder and bathed the wound with a clean cotton cloth.

Robert looked at her face lovingly while she rebandaged his shoulder. When she finished, Robert took hold of her hands and pulled her onto his lap. At first Virginia resisted slightly, but as he continued to look softly into her eyes, she submitted to his gentle kiss.

At the end of the kiss, Robert said softly and reverently, "In Africa you would be a princess."

Virginia traced the subtle lines on Robert's face with her hand.

"If ever anyone was meant to be a prince…" she began.

Later that same night, back in his room lit dimly with a single kerosene lamp, Robert removed his jacket, tossing it onto the bed. His small room was neat and orderly, with stacks of papers and books all around. His desk, despite its small size, was the central focus of the room, equipped with an ink well, a blotter, and a composition book. Robert stepped over to the desk and picked up a carved wooden statue of an African warrior.

In the subdued light, the shadows on the statue's face seemed to give it a life of its own. He stroked the wood and stared into the warrior's eyes trying to imagine how it must feel to live your life as totally your own man. Sitting down at the desk, Robert put the statue back in its place and picked up the pen. He opened the composition book and began to write. The only sound was the scratching of his pen.

Wednesday, 18 July 1900

The thoughts that swirl around in my mind sometimes seem to be pulling me down into a pit, like after talking with the foreman today. A very dark, deep pit. I get caught up in these thoughts at times and don't know how to pull away and get back to my life. When those thoughts grab hold of me, they start repeating themselves over and over, not letting any light into the pit that's sucking me in. They tell me, "No!" They say, "You are not unfettered. You don't have the power to break the chains that shackle you." Those evil thoughts tell me, "You cannot do it."

I mostly can take a quick grab at the edge of that pit and pull myself out. When I do, I throw myself out of the whirlpool of thoughts that suck me down. Then it is like I am looking at those thoughts from the outside and see them for what they are...anger, hurt, shame and perhaps, most scary of all, doubt. I cannot doubt myself or what I work so hard to have.

I remember Pa talking about the mule hooked up to the plow. That mule could work hard all day but still be free. That is what I am. A hard-working man, but a free man. I am not afraid of work. I am afraid of the thoughts that try to pull me down into the darkness of that pit. I am so close to the freedom Africa can bring me. Total freedom, not just a taste of it here and there or what I feel inside. Freedom on the outside that matches the freedom I feel within my heart and soul. I will live to see that day.

And I say goodnight to a day that had it all— bad, good, and everything in between. But at least it ended on a very fine note...Miss Virginia Banks.

Robert set his pen down, closed his composition book, and sat back in his chair with a gentle smile on his relaxed face. He had seen a new side to Virginia tonight, a side that made him like her even more. Robert was impressed with her vision for the future and began the first thoughts about what a life together could mean.

Chapter 7

Mid-morning, Thursday, 19 July 1900, New Orleans

The wharf bustled with fishermen untangling nets, steam hissing from barges, and random shouts between crewmen from one boat to the next. Work had begun for the longshoremen as they loaded and unloaded the ships and barges. Gulls swooped down and picked at dead fish left lying on the dock.

Robert approached the waterfront with his head down until the inescapable odor of fish smacked him in the face. He looked up and started searching for Lenard. When he saw the young man, he was sitting among a group of men he recognized. Robert picked up his pace. The 'gang'—Hollering John, Can Can Jimmie, Deadeye Dick, and Lenard—sat around several pilings. As Robert got closer, he could hear one of the men telling a tall tale. At its conclusion, the men howled with laughter. Jimmie began a story as Robert reached the group. He sat down beside Lenard and listened.

"That weren't nothin', Deadeye," Can Can Jimmie said. "Did I ever tell you the one 'bout the time I testified in court against my cousin for shootin' at me?"

The group's other men grumbled in recognition.

"Well, the lawyer," Can Can continued, "he said to me, 'You say that when the defendant pulled his gun, you began to run. How did you know that he was shooting at you?' And I said, 'I heard the gun fire, and I heard the bullet when it done went past me.' Then the lawyer asked, 'Are you absolutely sure that you heard the bullet pass you?' And I said, 'Yes, I'm absolutely sure I heard the bullet go past, 'cause I heard it twice.'"

Deadeye Dick, obligingly, asked with exaggerated surprise, "You heard the bullet twice? How on earth could that be?"

"That's just what the lawyer asked," Can Can answered. "So I told him, just like I'm tellin' you, 'It was like this—I heard the bullet when it flew past me, and I heard it again when I passed it!'"[12]

All the men howled again with laughter, Robert included.

Hollering John, ready to move on, said, "Enough of them lies. Deadeye, give me a note on that harp. Can Can, see if you can keep up with me."

Deadeye took out a harmonica and played three blues lines. Hollering John tapped along with his foot and came in on the beat.

> My momma tole me, my daddy tole me
> too,
> My momma tole me, my daddy tole me
> too,
> Everybody grins in yo' face, son,
> ain't no friend to you.

"Take it, Jimmie," John spoke out. Can Can, without missing a beat, began singing.

> When I had money, had friends fo' miles
> aroun',

When I had money, had friends fo' miles
aroun',
Now ain't got no money, friends cannot
be found.

"Tell it!" Lenard shouted. Hollering John picked up on the song.

When you got a dollar in [New
Orleans],
you got lots of friends,
When you got a dollar in [New
Orleans],
you got lots of friends,
But when you broke 'n' hungry,
that's where your friendships end.

Can Can's voice cut in, keeping up the tune.

When you lose yo' money, baby,
don't you lose yo' mind,
When you lose yo' money, baby,
don't you lose yo' mind,
You must remember all gamblers git
broke sometime.[13]

Hollering John carried on singing as Deadeye stopped playing the harmonica. His voice was sad and slow, filled with his life's woes.

I'm goin' to the river,
take my rockin' chair,

Goin' to the river,
take my rockin' chair,
If the blues overcome me,
I'll rock on away from here.[14]

"Rock us away, Deadeye!" Hollering John directed.

As Deadeye went into a blues solo on his harmonica, Robert nudged Lenard and motioned him away from the group. "I've got a few days off from work, Lenard," Robert began, "and I'm heading back to Mississippi."

"To see your family?" Lenard asked.

"Wish I could," Robert answered, "but not this trip. There's another matter I have to clear up. I need to see a man I used to work for. I got a letter from him yesterday saying he could meet me tomorrow."

"Not in any trouble, are ya'?" Lenard asked, slightly worried.

Robert smiled and tried to reassure his young friend. "None I can't handle. The reason I came looking for you is that I'd like you to stay in my room…keep an eye on things while I'm gone, if you don't mind."

"No problem," Lenard answered. "I'm between rooms now anyway."

"Good," Robert said. "I appreciate it. I'll be back the day after tomorrow, Sunday morning at the latest."

Lenard hesitated, a bit embarrassed. "Do you mind if I borrow one of your books? I figur' if I get better at readin', I'll up my chances of findin' a better job."

"Sure," Robert said, smiling at Lenard. "Just be careful not to break any bindings."

Lenard said quickly, “Thanks, and I’ll take real good care of the place. And you have a safe trip.”

Robert patted Lenard on the back. “I’ll try. And thanks, Les.” Robert waved to the gang and shouted, “See you later, guys.”

The gang responded in unison, “See ya, Buster!”

The steam from the train engines at New Orleans’ main depot intensified the late morning’s heat and upped the humidity tenfold it seemed. Whites and blacks mingled on the platform, but they entered separate compartments on the train.

When Robert arrived at the station, there was much commotion. He pushed his way toward the noise, and he bumped into Thomas O’Malley, who was also trying to reach the scene. New Orleans’ policeman, Patrolman Mora, rough-handled a young black man Robert recognized, Lewis Forstall. Robert moved to help Lewis, but the man he’d bumped stopped him by stepping in front of Robert.

“What’s going on here, Mora?” Thomas O’Malley demanded.

“Nothing to say, O’Malley,” Mora responded, “until the Captain gets here.”

At that moment, Mora’s superior, Captain John T. Day, arrived on the scene and took charge. He was a tall, husky man with a moustache and a very commanding presence.

“Report,” Captain Day directed Mora.

Holding on to Lewis, who stopped struggling when Captain Day arrived, Mora said, "This boy went into a compartment for whites only. He attempted to harm that woman over there." Mora pointed to a middle-aged white woman who looked very frightened. When Mora pointed to her, O'Malley hurried over to the woman. "I haven't taken her statement yet," Mora clarified, "but this boy denies it."

"You go talk to the woman while I question the suspect," Day instructed Mora.

Mora approached the woman as O'Malley returned to Day and Lewis. He caught Lewis mid-sentence, pleading desperately. "...didn't know it was for whites, I swear! And I didn't lay a finger on that woman. When I got on the train, she just screamed!"

"The woman admits he didn't touch her, Captain Day," O'Malley quickly stated.

"And just when did you join the force, O'Malley?" Captain Day asked sarcastically.

Mora stepped back to Captain Day, Lewis, and O'Malley. Robert remained out of the scene but listened intently.

Captain Day turned to Mora and asked, "What does the woman have to say?"

Mora read his notes from a small notebook. "She said, 'I was sitting in my seat when this horrid beast came in with a threatening look on his face. I wasn't about to wait for him to lay his filthy hands on me so I screamed.' When the witness was asked if the accused assaulted her, she responded, 'Given the chance, I'm sure he would have.' When asked for a simple yes or no, she said, 'No'."

Lewis, clearly relieved, said to Day, "See, Cap'n. I'm telling the truth!"

Captain Day hesitated. "Well, a mistake is possible," he finally stated then laughed. "I wouldn't be surprised if one of these days we'll have to put up signs to keep coloreds in their place."

O'Malley, a bit too eagerly, asked the Captain, "Does that mean you'll let him go?"

Captain Day responded, speaking in full seriousness to Lewis, "With a warning. Boy, you be more careful next time and make sure you're in the right place before you go traipsing into the wrong compartment."

Lewis, lowering his head, said with subservience, "Yes, sir. I promise, sir."

With a good-natured slap on the back, Captain Day let Lewis go. As Lewis moved away, he caught Robert's eye, and they looked at one another for a moment. Lewis held Robert's eye and gave him a quick nod and subtle grin.

A man standing behind the woman Lewis had been accused of attacking left her side and followed after Lewis. O'Malley, always a thorough journalist, questioned Mora while taking notes. He saw that Lewis was moving away, and O'Malley went after him.

Once the altercation seemed fully over, Robert moved to stand in a line of black people boarding the train, telling himself to step away from the angry thoughts swirling around the pit.

Robert disembarked from the train late that afternoon. He saw groups of white men running toward the center of town. Robert proceeded to the courthouse, which was in the town square. He noticed that some of the white men were looking at him and pointing. Sensing trouble, Robert carefully removed his Colt .45 from the back of his belt, which was covered by his overcoat, and placed the pistol in his right-hand coat pocket. He walked closer to the courthouse, staying on the fringes of the crowd that was gathering on the courthouse steps and spilling into the road.

Judge Chrisman appeared at the top of the steps. The crowd jeered at him. The judge shouted to be heard over the rabble. "Quiet down. Quiet down! If you'll hold on one cotton-pickin' minute, we can work this out!"

The mob quieted down enough to hear the judge.

Continuing to speak loudly, Judge Chrisman implored the crowd, "If you'll just let the law take its course, justice will be done."

A man in the middle of the crowd shouted, "The only justice is at the end of a rope. Turn him over to us!" Shouts of agreement came from the crowd.

Judge Chrisman responded with anger. "The only way you'll get the prisoner is over my dead body," the judge shouted.

Another man in the crowd responded, "That can be arranged!"

A middle-aged white man on the far edge of the crowd waved his rifle in the air. “Don’t tempt us, Judge Chrisman!” he warned.

At these threats, Judge Chrisman pulled a pistol out from under his robe. He shot the pistol into the air. Stillness came over the crowd. The judge boomed out with his deep voice. “If I go, I’m takin’ a few of you with me!” Judge Chrisman declared. “Now move aside and let me through.” The Judge descended the steps with his pistol aimed in front of him. The crowd separated for him to pass. A few men cocked their rifles and aimed them at the judge, but other men kept them from firing. Once through the crowd, Judge Chrisman hurried to the large fire bell in the town square and rang it loudly.

An older white man on the edge of the crowd said to the others around him, “The sheriff is bound to hear the bell and send back-ups for the Judge.” The others nodded in agreement, and the crowd members closest to the Judge began to disperse.

A younger white man holding a rifle declared, “That nigger ain’t worth white man’s blood. Let’s get out of here.” Members of the mob began to leave the town square. Soon there were only very small clusters of men left. The Judge continued to ring the bell.

Morning, Friday, 20 July 1900, Hazlehurst Courthouse, Mississippi

Robert sat in the back of the courtroom with his hat resting on his knees. An elderly white man in dungarees, Mr. Bryant, sat next to Robert. Judge Chrisman sat behind his bench at the front of the courtroom.

The bailiff stood and announced to the courtroom, “Will Mr. Curtis Robertson approach the bench?”

Robert walked toward the bench and stood before Judge Chrisman.

Reading from a report he held, Judge Chrisman said, “It says here, Mr. Robertson, that in August of eighteen and ninety-eight you were accused of selling liquor in a dry county. At that time you were arraigned and pleaded guilty.” The Judge looked directly at Robert. “I seem to recall that I fined you forty dollars,” the Judge said, “and you gave me your assurance that if I let you go, you would work to pay back the money. Have you finally come to pay the fine?”

Robert held his hat in his hand and looked up at Judge Chrisman. “No, Your Honor,” Robert stated.

Surprised, the Judge said, “No? You do realize that I can still put you in jail for this offense.”

“Yes, Your Honor,” Robert quickly answered. He continued to speak with respect, “If I may, I would please like to explain.”

“Seeing as you’ve dared to show your face after two years,” the Judge commented, “the least I can do is hear you out. Go on.”

Without hesitation, Robert said, “I would like to change my plea to ‘not guilty,’ Your Honor.”

There were murmurings in the courtroom, and Judge Chrisman banged his gavel. “Order,” he shouted.

Looking back at Robert, he said, "This is highly irregular, Mr. Robertson. Would you care to explain yourself?"

"Yes, Your Honor. And thank you," Robert said. "Two years ago when I was arrested, I had returned to Mississippi for the summer. Before that time I was living in New Orleans. I live there now as well. I came back to spend some time with my parents in Pine Bluff. It had been over a year since I'd seen them. While I was here, I worked at different jobs, mainly as a farm hand. But work was scarce in Copiah…that's where my family lives…so I came to this county hoping to find work. I needed to earn my fare back to New Orleans. Anyway, at the time I was arrested I was working for Mr. Bryant, that man sitting in the back row."

Robert turned and nodded toward Mr. Bryant, who shyly raised his hand. Robert looked back up at the Judge and continued to explain. "Your Honor, I couldn't be the man who sold that liquor because the day I was accused of selling it, I never left Mr. Bryant's farm. For that matter, I worked beside him all day."

Exasperated, Judge Chrisman asked, "Then why on Earth did you plead guilty?"

"If I could explain, Your Honor," Robert said.

"I sure wish you would!" the Judge said with a bit more curiosity than impatience.

Robert stood up straighter and said, "The day I supposedly sold that liquor, Mr. Bryant and I were building fences together from about seven a.m. until nearly eight that night. The witness who said I sold him the moonshine claimed he bought it from me around four o'clock in the afternoon."

Judge Chrisman interrupted Robert and addressed the bailiff, "Call Mr. Bryant up here."

The bailiff announced, "Will Mr. Bryant approach the bench?"

Mr. Bryant stood and walked up to the front of the courtroom to stand beside Robert.

Addressing Mr. Bryant, Judge Chrisman asked, "Do you verify what Mr. Robertson says?"

Nodding, Mr. Bryant answered, "Yes. I do, Your Honor."

Judge Chrisman asked, "But it's been over two years. How could you be sure of the date?"

Mr. Bryant pulled a small notebook out from his dungarees' pocket and opened it while saying, "I keep records of everything that goes on at the farm. On August third, 1898, Curtis here and me was putting in fences along the east edge of my pasture just like he said."

In full exasperation, Judge Chrisman demanded, "Why in heaven's name did you wait so long to tell me this? Why didn't you appear with Mr. Robertson when he was brought to trial before?"

Mr. Bryant looked down at the floor and shuffled his feet slightly.

Robert put his hand on Mr. Bryant's shoulder for a moment then let it drop. He looked up at the Judge and said, "Your Honor, it wasn't Mr. Bryant's fault. When the sheriff came out for me two days later, I didn't want to cause any trouble for Mr. Bryant. You see, his wife had been sick for quite a while, and the day before she had taken a turn for the worse. I came on with the sheriff, telling Mr. Bryant I had business in town. When I heard the charges, I figured the easiest thing to do was plead guilty and go back to work for Mr. Bryant to earn the money for the fine. When I got back to the farm, I found out that Mrs. Bryant had passed away. Mr. Bryant couldn't afford to keep me on, what with the funeral expenses, so I took my back wages and headed back to New Orleans hoping to find a new job there and mail the fine once I put forty dollars together."

Silence filled the courtroom for a moment, interrupted by the Judge asking Mr. Bryant. "Do you verify Mr. Robertson's story?"

"Yes, sir," Mr. Bryant answered. He then said more confidently, "Curtis here is a good worker, and I wish he done told me back then he was in trouble. I would've helped him out then, but I'm glad I can now. He wrote me about a month ago telling me all about it and saying he wanted to clear his name. I said, 'Sure.'"

Judge Chrisman shuffled a small stack of papers and said, "I wish he'd asked for your help back then. This is all highly irregular. I'm not sure there's ever been a precedent. Then again…"

The Judge looked straight at Robert and said, "I've never hesitated being the one to set the precedent so, Mr. Robertson, if you're willing to pay the court costs of ten dollars, I'll change the verdict for bootlegging to 'not guilty.' And I'll drop the charges for failure to pay the fine."

Robert smiled up at the Judge and said, "Yes, Your Honor. Thank you, Your Honor." He quickly turned to Mr. Bryant. "And you too."

Robert and Mr. Bryant shook hands. Judge Chrisman pounded his gavel once and declared, "Dismissed."

Chapter 8

Afternoon, Sunday, 22 July 1900, New Orleans

Virginia entered her apartment's sitting room from the bedroom. She was dressed in her finest clothes. Her roommate, Ernestine, sat on the couch darning a pair of stockings. She looked up when Virginia entered.

"Ernestine, how do I look?" Virginia asked, twirling around with her arms spread wide.

Ernestine put her sewing down in her lap and tilted her head to the right, asking, "Where you going all dressed up like that?"

"Robert invited me to dinner with his sister and her family," Virginia answered. "He just got back from Mississippi and said that now it was okay for him to court me properly."

Ernestine picked up her sewing and asked, "What's that supposed to mean? Haven't you two been seeing each other for some time now?"

Virginia laughed and said, "You're right, but I've got this feeling that maybe Robert is wanting to pick up the pace. You can tell a man is serious when he invites you for dinner with his family."

"You're not telling me that you're feeling more serious about this man?" Ernestine asked with concern.

"I know that I like him and that he's going places," Virginia stated.

"Yeah, going to jail maybe," Ernestine laughed then turned serious again. "Do you even know where he's working these days? For all you know, he's one of them nasty roustabouts from down on the river."

"He is not!" Virginia declared defensively. "He works at a sawmill for your information."

"Sawmill?" Ernestine gasped. "Now what kind of job is that? Why do you waste your time with some down-home country boy? Why don't you find yourself some decent sort of man, like one of them Creoles with money. You're certainly pretty enough."

"I don't care about money," Virginia stated. "Robert has something more. He's got a vision."

Ernestine threw her head back and laughed. "Oh, child. No vision is going to buy you what you like wearing. Or is he planning to dress you in some African grass skirt?"

Remaining defensive, Virginia declared, "They don't wear grass skirts in Liberia."

Ernestine challenged Virginia somewhat disbelievingly. "Are you telling me that you'd take off clear across the ocean to some jungle with that man?"

Virginia hesitated then said, "I doubt it's a jungle....I don't know....Africa does seem strange."

"Strange?" Ernestine said. "Why I bet they haven't even heard about shoes over there. If you have any sense, Ginny, my friend, you'll forget about that Mr. Charles and stay focused on our goal. We'll get into nursing school, and then we'll find ourselves some good-looking doctors with money in their pockets!"

This comment angered Virginia, who quickly responded, "My interest in nursing isn't to get married, and, Ernestine, you've never even met Robert. Don't go judging him without knowing what makes him special. And I've changed my mind. If Robert asks me to go to Africa with him, I will!"

The home of Alice Pittman, Robert's younger sister, was filled with the warm smells of country cooking and the happy sounds of two rambunctious children. Her husband, Earl, was a skilled carpenter, and their home was furnished with tables, chairs, and cabinets he had crafted. Placed on top of the mantel and bookcases were various pictures of Alice's and Earl's family—children, parents, brothers, and sisters. Handmade quilts and afghans adorned the couch and chairs, and a well-worn rocking chair sat on a braided rug in front of the fireplace. While not middle-class, the Pittmans were certainly above the poverty level. Hearing a knock, Alice went to the door and opened it to greet Robert and Virginia.

She gave Robert a big hug and said, "Oh, Robert, you've been such a stranger lately."

"I know, Alice," Robert responded. "And I'm sorry. I'd like you to meet Virginia Banks. Virginia, this is my sister, Alice."

Alice shook Virginia's hand and said, "Welcome, Virginia. It's so nice to finally meet you." She stepped back to let Robert and Virginia enter. "You two come on in and sit down," Alice invited before turning to shout into the house. "Earl! Children! Robert's here."

Mariah, a six-year-old, and Luke, a three-year-old named for another of Robert's brothers, ran into the entranceway and threw themselves into Robert's arms. In unison, the children shouted with glee, "Uncle Robert!"

Robert hugged both children then tossed Luke up on his shoulders. He turned to Virginia and said, "Virginia, this is Mariah, and this little fellow up here is Luke."

Luke said defiantly, "I'm not little!"

"Pardon me!" Robert corrected. "This big fellow is Mr. Lucas Pittman."

Virginia smiled and looked at Robert's niece and nephew. "I'm pleased to meet you both."

Mariah crossed her arms and asked Virginia quite seriously, "Are you going to marry my Uncle Robert?"

Abashed, Alice said, "Mariah! You come into the kitchen and help me with dinner." To Robert and Virginia she said, "You two go on in the living room and sit down. Earl should be here in a minute. Here he is!"

Earl, about Robert's age only slightly shorter and smaller, entered the hallway. He shook hands with Robert and took Luke down from Robert's shoulders. He led his guests into the living room.

Luke proudly told his daddy, "She's Miss Sippi!"

The adults laughed.

"Her name's Virginia," Robert corrected his nephew.

Earl shook Virginia's hand and said, "Pleased to meet you."

"Thank you, Mr. Pittman. Robert tells me you made all this furniture. It's just lovely."

Earl beamed and said, "Thank you. And please call me Earl."

Mariah marched into the room from the kitchen and said, "Mama says you should come to the table now."

The three adults and two children went into the next room, a large kitchen with a wooden table and chairs to the side. They sat around the table and bowed their heads. Earl prayed out loud. "The Lord has seen fit to bless us with a table full of good food, family, and friends. For this we are truly thankful. May He also bless our kinfolk not with us today, and keep them safe. Amen."

"Amen," the family repeated in unison.

The family passed around the food and filled their plates, all the while talking with one another.

"How's your trip to Africa coming along, Robert?" Earl asked.

"I should finish paying the forty dollars required to go by the end of the year," Robert answered then added, "Work is steady at the sawmill."

Alice, feeling a bit upset, asked, "So soon? It's already July. That's only six months! I don't want you to go that soon."

Robert smiled tenderly at his sister and said, "I doubt we'll set sail in the winter. My guess is that a ship will head out in about a year, during the summer. Besides, I won't be ready to leave until then."

"Why's that?" Earl asked his brother-in-law.

Robert smiled at Virginia and said, "I'm saving up my money for something else too."

With a slight smile on her lips, Virginia glanced at Robert. The family continued to converse as Alice served pecan pie for dessert—the scene of a family in all its love and closeness.

When they finished, Virginia helped Alice clear the table while the men and children moved back into the living room. Robert sat in the rocking chair, and Earl pulled up a cane chair across from him, offering Robert a cigar. Luke crawled into Robert's lap, and Mariah went to her father.

She asked, "Will you tell us a story, Uncle Robert?"

He asked a question in response. "Which one do you want to hear?"

Luke answered with the full enthusiasm only a child can muster. "The Knee-High Man!"

"The Knee-High Man?" Robert asked his nephew. "Surely you're tired of that one by now. I tell it every time I come over."

"Please tell it again," Mariah begged.

"Yeah!" Luke chimed in. "Again!"

Robert laughed. "Okay," he said. "You convinced me."

Alice and Virginia entered the room and sat on the couch to listen.

"Well, as you know," Robert began, "this is a true story. Your granddaddy told it to me when I was a boy, and his daddy told it to him."

Mariah stated seriously, "He was a slave, wasn't he?"

Robert smiled at Mariah and said, "That's right. As you know, my mama and pa—your granny and grandpa—live near a swamp, and in that swamp lives a knee-high man. He's always wanting to be big instead of little. So he says to himself, 'I is gonna ax the biggest thang in this here neighborhood how I's can get to be sizeable.'"

The kids laughed at their uncle's affected accent.

Robert continued. "So he goes to see Mr. Horse. The knee-high man asks him, 'Mr. Horse, I come to get you to tell me how to get big like you is.' Mr. Horse, he says, 'You eat a whole lot of corn and then you run 'round and 'round and 'round 'til you been about twenty miles, and after a while you'll be as big as me.' So the knee-high man, he did all that Mr. Horse told him. And the corn made his stomach hurt, and running so much made his legs hurt, and trying made his mind hurt. And he gets smaller and smaller."

Mariah and Luke giggled as Robert continued.

"Then the knee-high man sits in his house and studies how come Mr. Horse helped him none. And he says to himself, 'I is gonna go see Brer Bull.' So he goes to see Brer Bull and he says, 'Brer Bull, I come to ax you to tell me how to get big like you.' And Brer Bull, he says, 'You eat a whole lot of grass and then bellow and bellow and the first thing you know you'll be big like me.' And the knee-high man did all that Brer Bull told him. And the grass made his stomach hurt, and the bellowing made his neck hurt, and the thinking made his mind hurt. And he gets…"

Mariah and Luke finished the sentence in unison. "…smaller and smaller!"

Robert picked up on the story.

"Then the knee-high man he sits in his house and he studies how come Brer Bull ain't done him no good. After a while, he hears old Mr. Hoot Owl way down in the swamp preaching that bad people is sure gonna have bad luck. Then the knee-high man says to himself, 'I's gonna ax Mr. Hoot Owl how I's can get to be sizeable.'"

Robert paused before picking up on the story, thinking the kids were going to chime in, but they remained mesmerized.

"And he goes to see wise old Mr. Hoot Owl. And Mr. Hoot Owl says, 'What you want to be big for?' And the knee-high man says, 'I wants to be big so when I's gets in a fight, I can whup 'sted of get whupped.' And Mr. Hoot Owl asks, 'Anybody ever try to pick a scrap with you?' The knee-high man thinks a minute then answers, 'Naw.' And Mr. Hoot Owl says, 'Well, then, you ain't got no cause to fight, and you ain't got no cause to be more sizeable than you is.' The knee-high man says, 'But I's wants to be big so I's can see a far ways.' Mr. Hoot Owl, he says, 'Can't you climb a tree and see a far ways when you climb to the top?' The knee-high man, he says, 'Yeah, I guess so.' Mr. Hoot Owl says, 'Then you ain't got no cause to be bigger in the body, but you sho' is got cause to be…'"

Robert, Mariah, and Luke said loudly in unison, "'bigger in the BRAIN!'"[15]

The children howled with laughter, and the adults smiled fondly at the memory of their own childhood stories. Virginia looked lovingly at Robert, seeing a more rounded picture of this man in her life.

Evening, Sunday, 22 July 1900, New Orleans

After Robert and Virginia returned to her house, Virginia opened the front door for them. As they entered the hallway, Virginia's landlady, Mrs. Cooley, startled Robert and Virginia. Mrs. Cooley, a middle-aged white woman dressed in a house robe and night cap, stepped in the hallway, immediately ill at ease. She spoke to her tenant. "Virginia, who is this man, and what is he doing here at this time of night?"

Virginia stepped between Robert and her landlady. "Mrs. Cooley, this is my gentleman friend, Mr. Charles. He walked me home from dinner, and I've just invited him in for coffee."

Robert removed his hat and nodded at Mrs. Cooley, saying, "Good evening, ma'am."

Still nervous, Mrs. Cooley declared, "You know full well, Virginia, that I don't allow men in this house after nine o'clock. It's nearly ten now."

Virginia, quick to appease Mrs. Cooley, said, "I assure you, Mrs. Cooley, that he'll only stay a half hour. No longer."

Mrs. Cooley took a stronger stance, not backing down, "When you moved into that apartment, Virginia, you agreed to the rules. Besides, there's no way I can fall asleep knowing he's in this house. If he does not leave immediately, I will have to call the police!"

Trying to calm the situation, Robert said, "There's no need for the police, Mrs. Cooley. I'll leave, but could I have just a moment alone with Miss Banks?"

"You can go back outside to talk, Virginia," Mrs. Cooley answered adamantly, not addressing Robert at all. "I want him out of this house right now."

Virginia, knowing any more arguing was ill advised, said with deference, "Yes, ma'am."

Mrs. Cooley waited until Virginia and Robert went out the front door before going upstairs. Outside the house, Virginia walked Robert back out to the sidewalk. They held hands.

Smiling, Virginia said, "There's a drugstore up on the corner. Stendel's. It's open until midnight. Go wait there for about half an hour, then come back. If Mrs. Cooley's light is out, tap on my front window, and I'll let you in."

Robert said hesitantly, "I don't want to cause any trouble for you…or for me either."

Virginia gave Robert a coy smile and said, "The only trouble you'll be in is if you don't come back here."

Robert kissed Virginia lightly on the cheek and walked off in the direction of Stendel's. Virginia headed back to her house, but before entering she caught sight of Mrs. Cooley peeking out from behind her upstairs' bedroom drapes.

Inside Stendel's drugstore, Robert sat at the counter with a cup of coffee as two patrolmen, Mora and

Cantrelle, entered. Cantrelle beckoned the waiter, Ira, working behind the counter.

"Ira," Cantrelle said, "I need to call in a report to the precinct. Can I use that contraption?" he asked, pointing to Stendel's Candlestick phone, one of the few telephones in the neighborhood.

"Sure," Ira answered. "Come on around the counter. Can I get you fellas anything tonight?"

"Just a coupla' cups of coffee, Ira," Mora answered.

Ira poured two cups of coffee and put them on the counter where Mora sat. Cantrelle bent over the phone and talked into the mouthpiece while holding the phone's neck with his left hand. He held the earpiece up to his right ear. Not used to a phone, Cantrelle practically shouted as he talked into the mouthpiece.

Mora glanced at Robert and looked at him suspiciously. Robert paid for his coffee and left the drugstore. Mora watched him as he went.

Robert exited Stendel's, and when he reached Virginia's house, he looked around to make sure no one was watching. The upstairs lights were off so Robert tapped quietly on Virginia's front window. A few seconds later the front door opened, and Robert slipped inside.

Virginia stood in her dimly lit bedroom wearing a modest dressing gown. Robert handed her his overcoat, and as she put it across the back of a chair, Virginia noticed the Colt .45 in the large right-hand pocket.

Frightened, she held the coat out to Robert, and asked coldly, "What is this?"

She pulled the Colt out of the pocket and let the coat drop to the floor. Robert, who had turned to take a look at Virginia's room, stopped cold when he saw her holding the Colt. With one long stride, Robert reached Virginia and grabbed the gun from her.

"Never touch that gun again!" Robert commanded.

Robert's anger frightened Virginia even more. She started to tremble and cry. Robert put the gun down on the dresser, stepped to Virginia, took her in his arms, and stroked her loosened hair.

Robert tried to shush her crying and said gently, "I'm sorry, princess. I didn't mean to scare you, but when I saw you holding that gun, all I could think about was you getting hurt."

Virginia pushed herself away from Robert somewhat angrily and looked up into his face. "Why do you even have a gun?" she demanded.

Robert stepped back from Virginia, somewhat surprised at this question. "It's only for protection," he explained, "in case I come across a wild dog walking home from the sawmill. A friend of mine was bitten a couple of months ago. His leg got very infected, and he died."

Virginia challenged this explanation. "Have you ever used it on a man? Have you ever killed anyone?" she asked.

Robert crossed his arms in front of his chest, taking a more defensive stance. "Not killed anyone," Robert answered, "but I have shot at a man or two. But only after they shot at me. And not here in New Orleans. Back in Mississippi a while ago. But I will defend myself if I'm attacked."

Robert's words didn't calm Virginia. Robert uncrossed his arms and let his body relax in hopes of helping her feel more at ease. As he began to take a step toward her, she took two steps back. Robert stopped and said more seriously, "Listen, Virginia, these are dangerous times. A man has to protect himself. You can't always know who your friends are. The only one you can really trust is yourself. I don't go out looking for trouble, but if it comes to me I'm going to be ready. I have no intention of feeling a rope around my neck."

Virginia immediately put one hand to her neck, visibly trembling again. "Talk like that scares me, Robert," she said. "You say you can only trust yourself. Does that mean you don't trust me?"

Robert gently approached Virginia and took her in his arms again. She continued to tremble, and new, silent tears rolled down her mocha-brown cheeks.

Robert stroked her hair and said, "No, princess, I trust you totally, but I want to protect you too. I don't want to see you get hurt. You can't put all your trust in someone else. Ultimately, we each have to follow our own instincts. This is a tough world to live in, but it's all we've got and we have to keep on living."

Robert felt Virginia relax into his arms. He kissed the tears from her cheeks, and soon Virginia responded to the loving and returned his kisses. After a few moments, Robert lifted his head and looked down on Virginia's upturned face. He cupped the right side of her face with his strong left hand and smiled lovingly at this remarkable woman. Her beauty showed strength and vulnerability, independence and empathy, intelligence and natural spirit. She was unlike any woman Robert had ever known, and he wanted to keep her in his life.

"Will you stay over?" Virginia asked quietly.

"I would love to stay with you tonight more than anything in the world," Robert answered, "but I will not put you at risk, or myself."

"But Ernestine works the night shift at the hospital tonight," Virginia said. "You can be gone before daybreak."

"What about the landlady?" Robert asked.

Virginia smiled softly, "I can handle Mrs. Cooley. Besides, I was surprised she was even up when we got back here after dinner. It's usually lights out for her by 8:30. When she does stay up that late, she won't be out of bed before nine!"

Both Robert and Virginia chuckled before Robert turned serious again. Robert opened his mouth to speak, but Virginia placed her index finger over his lips to shush him. "It's not like we've never been down this road before," Virginia said. "And I can take care of myself. Any man who thinks he can take advantage of me will be limping for a few days."

Robert instinctively pulled his front away from Virginia a little bit. Both laughed. "Don't you worry, Robert," Virginia assured him. "I know human anatomy and how it works. I also know WHEN it works, and tonight is our night."

Virginia stood on her tiptoes and gently kissed Robert, who picked her up and carried her to the bed. Unlike his night with Ruby, Robert found love and tenderness amidst the passion with Virginia.

Early Morning, Monday, 23 July 1900, New Orleans

Just before first light, Robert and Virginia awakened in each other's arms and smiled at one another. "I'm going to be late for work if I don't hurry," Robert said. "This is my first day back since the 'accident', and I want to make sure the foreman doesn't think I'm not going to show."

"I don't go into work until late morning and work only a half day today," Virginia said.

Robert gave Virginia a gentle kiss on her cheek and swung his legs out of bed. He reached to the chair at the side of the bed and grabbed his pants. He pulled them on and stood up. He started putting on his shirt, when Virginia, still in bed, asked, "When will I see you again?" Then with a bit of hesitation, she asked, "Or will I? It had been almost five months since we last got together."

As he was putting on his shirt, Robert smiled down at Virginia and responded, "What do you think?"

"Well," Virginia started to say.

"There's no ifs, ands, or buts about it," Robert said. "You ain't gonna git rid of me that easy, girl!"

Both laughed as Robert leaned over Virginia and kissed her. Robert stood and grew more serious. "You asked me last night if I trusted you," Robert said. "I could ask the same of you. Do you trust me?" He paused to think for a moment then said, "I guess I need to prove myself."

"We've got plenty of time to prove it to each other," Virginia said. "I just want to know how you feel."

Robert smiled down at Virginia with the twinkle in his eyes that attracted her to him the first time they met. "I feel good!" he teased.

"You know that's not what I meant," she said. Virginia looked directly into Robert's eyes, the challenge to him spoken in her look.

Robert stood up straight and looked down at Virginia and said gently, "You've flown off with my heart, little bird, and I'm not going to ask for it back."

Robert put on his jacket and picked up his overcoat and hat. The pistol was still on the dresser. Robert walked over, picked it up, and put it back in his coat pocket. He smiled down at Virginia.

"I've got to hurry if I'm going to get home and change before work," Robert said, "I don't know when I'll get another day off, but when I do, I'll most definitely be taking you out for some good eats and dancing."

"I'll hold you to that," Virginia said, sitting up in bed and pulling the sheets and blankets up to her neck.

Robert laughed and smiled down at Virginia. "I have no doubt you will."

As Robert put his hat on to leave, Virginia said quietly, “I love you too, Robert.”

Robert blew Virginia a kiss before he turned and left the room. Virginia fell back on her pillows and sighed with contentment.

Chapter 9

Morning, Monday, 23 July 1900, New Orleans

Robert, now dressed in his work clothes, reported to the sawmill. As he approached the office, the foreman stepped out, holding his inevitable clipboard.

Seeing Robert, the foreman, said, “Oh, good, Charles, you’re back. How ya‘ feelin‘?”

Robert responded enthusiastically, “Fit as a fiddle, sir.”

“That’s good,” the foreman said. After a moment’s hesitation he continued, “Step on into the office a minute, will ya‘?”

Robert, led by the foreman, went into the office. The foreman motioned Robert into a chair, and he went to stand by his desk, setting the clipboard down. He fiddled with a stone paperweight and would not look directly at Robert.

To break the nervous silence, Robert said, “I’m anxious to start back to work today. Is my position on the cutting team still open?”

The foreman continued to hesitate. “Well, Robert,” he finally said. “That’s what I wanted to talk to you about. There’ve been some changes in the past coupla’ days.”

Robert shifted in his chair, not liking where this conversation seemed to be heading. “You mean you want me to work on another team?” Robert asked the foreman.

The foreman looked out the window and answered hesitantly, "Well, no, not exactly."

With a bit more than a hint of defiance Robert asked, "What, exactly, sir?"

The foreman paced in front of his desk then blurted out, "Damn it, Charles! While you were gone the company lost a very important order. Ya see, a huge load of timber was supposed to be delivered the day after you left, and it still hasn't gotten here. Now there's no way we can meet the deadline for the Winthrop order. He's got three buildings in the works so, of course, we had to tell him about the delay. He took his business to Norton's sawmill. They had enough in reserve to cover what Winthrop needed. We've been so busy lately that we couldn't even give him enough lumber for one building."

Robert stood up quickly. "What are you saying?" he asked.

The foreman stopped pacing and looked directly at Robert. "I'm sayin' I had to lay off a few hands," the foreman said. "Losin' that order meant we lost a lot of cash, and now we can't afford to keep so many people on. I really would like to keep you, Robert. You're one of my best workers. I wish I had more like you, but…"

Robert finished the foreman's sentence, "…but you're letting me go."

"'Fraid I have to, Robert," the foreman said. "No choice. It's nothing personal, understand."

Again, Robert grew very angry at being told he was losing his job but it was nothing personal. He stood and took a step toward the foreman then stopped. "No, sir, it never is," Robert stated. "When I was coming over here,

I saw Mickey slacking off near the unloading truck. Does that mean you haven't cut him?"

The foreman, growing a bit defensive, said, "That's right."

Robert took a step and leaned against the foreman's desk with two balled-up fists, ready to challenge his boss.

"But I've been here longer," Robert argued, "and you said yourself that I'm a better worker."

Stepping back from Robert, the foreman tried to explain. "After the trouble you had with Mickey, there was no way I could cut him and keep you," the foreman said. "It would've made for more trouble. I did it for your own good."

Robert finally let his anger show itself. "Begging your pardon, sir, but how do you know what's good for me?" he challenged. "What's good for me is a steady income. I can take care of Mickey, but I can't take care of myself if I'm not getting paid. Besides, it was Mickey who caused the trouble, not me."

Taken aback by Robert's anger, the foreman pulled himself up tall to confront Robert. "Look, Charles, this mill is lucky not to have a Negro problem. Everyone basically gets along fine, and I want to keep it that way. If I let Mickey go and kept you, lots of men around here might start causing trouble for the other colored workers."

"Negro problem?" Robert said bitterly. "It's not us with the problem."

"Easy, Robert," the foreman warned. "You're walking on thin ice."

Robert felt both so surprised and sure of what the foreman said to him that he couldn't hold back. "Us 'coloreds' have been walking on thin white ice all our lives," he declared.

Picking up his clipboard, the foreman figured it was time to wrap up this conversation before it got out of hand.

"Then you just better keep on walking lightly, else you gonna fall through, Robert."

Robert looked directly into the foreman's eyes and held his gaze for a moment before he said, "If I do, I might just take some of you with me." Robert stalked out of the office.

Robert walked quickly away, but to leave the sawmill he had to go right by the unloading trucks. Mickey was down off his truck, and he saw Robert approaching.

Shouting at Robert, Mickey said, "Hey, Sambo, bossman finally figured you out. He only wants real men working here."

Robert lunged at Mickey, knocking him to the ground and falling on top of the teenager. The two men wrestled in the dirt, but Robert was stronger. He was soon on top of Mickey, pounding the boy's face with his fists. It took three men to pull Robert off Mickey.

One of the men, a middle-aged black man named Horace, held on to both Robert's arms and spoke into Robert's ear with low tones, "Easy does it, Robert. You better get yourself outta here before some other whitey makes real trouble."

Robert shook Horace free, picked up his hat, stared down at Mickey, and turned away.

Shouting at Robert's back, Mickey said, "I'll kill you, nigger! I swear I'll kill you!

Robert walked into his room to find Lenard stretched out on one of the two single beds. Now that he could see the room in the full light of day, unlike earlier this morning when he'd come home to change clothes, Robert saw that it was in disarray. Robert looked around with disgust. He spoke angrily to Lenard, "I thought I told you to have this room cleaned up by the time I got home."

Lenard sat up quickly. "I didn't think you'd be home so soon. I planned on cleaning it up and moving out of here by five. Why you home so early?"

Robert busied himself, straightening the things on his desk. "I got laid off," Robert said, calming down a bit. "If you want to stay on here, you'd help me save on rent."

Lenard responded hesitantly, "Sure, if you don't mind. I'll try to be neater." Lenard had been reading one of Robert's books, and as he got off the bed, he tossed the book on the floor. This action was the last straw for Robert.

Robert yelled, "Pick that book up! Damn you, Les. Didn't I tell you to be careful with my books?"

Lenard, quite frightened, said, “I’m sorry, man,” and he reached to pick up the book.

“Give it to me!” Robert demanded.

Lenard handed Robert the book, but instead of taking the book Robert grabbed Lenard roughly by the collar.

“From now on, leave my things alone!” he yelled. Robert released Lenard, who took a step back, tripped, and fell on his bed. Robert carefully inspected the book’s spine and replaced it on the desk. When he turned around, he saw Lenard sitting on the bed hugging his knees and rocking slightly. Robert collapsed on the edge of the other bed, holding his face in his hands.

Afternoon, Monday, 23 July 1900, New Orleans

O’Malley stood at the bar inside Jordan’s Inn drinking a beer. Laborers were not off work yet so the barroom was fairly quiet. Two older black men played a game of billiards, and a younger black man picked a tune on a guitar at one of the tables. Robert entered Jordan’s Inn and approached the bar.

“Beer, Jordan,” he said to the bartender.

Jordan filled a mug from the tap and put it in front of Robert, who took a foamy first sip before smoothing the ends of his moustache. Jordan then stepped over to O’Malley.

“That’s the man I was telling you about,” Jordan said to the journalist.

"Thanks." O'Malley put a coin on the bar, picked up his beer, and walked over to Robert.

Thomas O'Malley stood beside Robert and said, "My name's O'Malley. I'm a journalist for the *Daily States*. I heard that people who are interested in going back to Africa sometimes hang around here."

Robert looked suspiciously at Thomas but didn't say anything. He took another long sip of his beer.

O'Malley continued to speak, "Jordan here tells me that you're interested in going back to Africa. To Liberia. I'm writing an article about the movement and would like to ask you a few questions. Would you mind?"

Robert asked guardedly, "What kind of questions?"

Trying to put Robert at ease, he said, "Just about your reasons for going, and what you hope to do once you're over there. Nothing else."

Robert, still worked up over the day, said, "You can ask, but I won't guarantee any answers."

"That's fine," O'Malley reassured Robert. "Would you like to sit down at one of the tables?"

Robert took a long couple of chugs and nearly drained the beer from his glass. Thomas said to the bartender, "Two more, please."

Jordan drew two more beers and put them in front of Robert and Thomas. He took the coins Thomas offered him. O'Malley picked up his beer and turned to the nearest table. "Let's move over to the table. That way I can take notes."

Robert grew suspicious again, and Thomas realized that the mention of notes was ill advised. "All I'd like to do is talk," O'Malley tried to reassure Robert. "I don't have to take notes. I just want to hear what you have to say."

Robert silently picked up his beer and walked over to a table. Thomas followed. Once they were seated, Thomas reached in his pocket for his notebook and pencil and started to take them out, a force of habit. Robert caught the move.

"I'll talk, but no notes," Robert said.

"I hear you," Thomas said, "but it would be good if I could quote you accurately."

"You can use the information I give you, but I don't want you quoting me," Robert stated definitively. "Or mentioning my name," he added.

Thomas held up two empty hands and said, "No notes and no identifying you. Promise."

"Don't expect me to trust you," Robert said. "Start asking questions, and I'll decide what I answer."

"Fair enough," O'Malley agreed.

Both he and Robert took long swallows of their beers. "When did you first think of going back to Africa?" Thomas asked when he set down his mug.

"In the first place, I'm not going back to Africa," Robert clarified. "I've never been there before."

"Good point," O'Malley agreed, then asked, "What started you thinking about moving there?"

"An uncle told me about it years ago, and when I got to New Orleans I heard more about the idea when I learned about the International Migration Society," Robert said, then paused before continuing. "In the past five years or so, it's seemed like the only solution."

"Solution to what?" Thomas asked.

"To living the kind of life I want," Robert answered.

The back-and-forth interview seemed to be picking up steam.

"And what kind of life is that?" O'Malley asked.

Robert didn't answer this last question, halting the interview's forward momentum. He took a long swallow of beer. After a few moments of awkward silence, Thomas made a statement meant to provoke an answer from Robert. "Some whites think that the Negroes are doing them a favor by going to Africa," he said.

Robert, who had taken a swallow from his beer, slammed the half-full mug down on the table, sloshing the golden brew. He said harshly, "If I ever get to Africa, the only favor I'm doing them is taking myself away before they push me too far!"

Robert stood up with force, toppling his chair over backwards. He stalked out of Jordan's bar without looking back. Thomas, angry with himself for his line of questioning, stood up, pushed his chair in, and walked around the table to put Robert's chair upright. He carried his empty mug and Robert's half full one over to the bar. "Excuse me, Jordan," O'Malley asked the bartender. "What was that man's name?"

"Only name I know for him is Buster," Jordan answered.

Robert let his anger settle down a bit as he walked back to his apartment. He bought a newspaper from a hawker on the street corner, folded it and stuck it under his arm. He continued walking down the street, turned left into an alleyway, and entered his room—the fourth door down the alley on his right.

Once in his room, Robert sat down at his desk to read the newspaper, the day's issue of *The Times-Democrat*. He started on page one, his attention caught by one of the headlines, "By the Use of Keyboards: Perfected Machines Which Operated Like a Typewriter, Transmits Dots and Dashes and at the Other End Reconvert Them Into Typewritten Messages."[16] Robert enjoyed reading about new inventions and progress, but today, having just lost his job, he couldn't settle down his thoughts.

As he flipped through the newspaper pages he came upon an article that was written by a local New Orleans doctor, Gustav Keitz, on "Compulsory School Education." Robert scanned the article, remembering the first part of the article that had been published by *The Times-Democrat* a week earlier. In that issue, Keitz had proposed that Negroes be deported to Cuba, Puerto Rico, and the Philippines to separate them from whites. These people would then receive a compulsory education in "mechanical" learning since it was "imitative", and that was the limit of a Negro's educational capabilites, according to Keitz. In this most recent article, Robert read, "Such an education, however, should be extended only to those who pledge themselves to deportation."[17]

It was one thing to plan on moving to another country for oneself, but to be forced out of the United States because of a white-perceived "Negro problem" sparked Robert's outrage. His grip on the newspaper tightened, and he threw it on the floor. He turned to a small stack of newspapers next to his desk and flipped through it until he found the 16 July 1900 issue of *The Times-Democrat*. He turned the pages until he saw the small header, "Compulsory School Education by Dr. Gustav Keitz."[18] Robert had read the article before, but he redirected his full attention to what Keitz was writing.

> "…while I don't want to wrong anybody, I shall certainly give expression to my honest opinion.
>
> "We owe the negro justice above everything else. We must remember that he is here not through his own choice, but through compulsion, he having been taken from his native home and transported to a strange land and among a strange race; and while his condition as a slave might favorably compare with his wild and unsettled existence in Africa, here, under existing conditions, he is certainly out of place. He is in a most unfortunate position, because he is unfitted for his former home and a misfit in the Caucasian race. This, however, does not signify that he should not be subject to the law of this country. Everybody, no matter who he is or what his virtues or vices are, has to live and act within the rules governing the land

in which he resides. Any infringement on the law will be punished, since the law cannot make an exception on account of a person's inferior mental development...

"The [Thirteenth, Fourteenth, and Fifteenth Amendments] are the basis of the ridiculous claim of social equality, and are responsible for the intricate complications in, and the incalculable injury to, the South....Everybody of average intelligence knows that social equality does not and cannot exist, even among the whites; how, then, can such an impossibility be effected between two races so vastly different in all essential points, in color, mental, moral and intellectual development, educability and 'previous condition?'

"No process known to science or demonstrated by experience can possibly reconcile such incongruities....

"The welfare and prosperity of a nation (or country) is based on the greatest good to the greatest number....

"The negro is in the minority, not only numerically but also as to quality, a two-fold reason why a greater sacrifice is not only expected but rightfully demanded of him....The race that offers the greater promise of future usefulness

> and higher attainments should receive first consideration. The most biased, most sanguine friend of the negro must admit that his future presents no encouraging prospects whatever; he gives no promise of a higher development than his present state, while the Caucasian has a bright future before him. The negro, on the contrary, has been a weight, a drag, a hindrance to progress and a source of discontent and political corruption in the State and community in which he resides.
>
> "That the negro cannot remain among the white people as he is now is becoming more and more apparent. He has been degenerating since the war; his crimes are becoming more frequent and more revolting....the fact that we are on the threshold of a race war cannot be denied....Medical men have discussed the problem and are agreed that the number of negroes should be reduced, and have suggested asexualization..."

At this declaration, Robert's face muscles grew taut with stress and tension. Beads of sweat appeared on his forehead. He finished reading the sentence.

> "…a measure that should be practiced at
> the earliest possible period of life."[19]

Robert's fury reached a crescendo. Throwing his head back, Robert screamed from the very depths of his soul. Reaching out for the nearest object, Robert grabbed the African statue and hurled it at the wall. The figure fell to the floor, leaving a large gash in the wall. The impact also left a noticeable crack down the center of the statue's face.

Chapter 10

Evening, Monday, 23 July 1900, New Orleans

Robert sat in his room dressed in a black jacket, white shirt with a green tie, and dark pants, ready to go out for the evening. He figured since he didn't have to go to work in the morning, he'd take Virginia out tonight—at least to hear some music at a club—while he still had some money. He was at his desk writing in his composition book when Lenard entered the room still wearing his day clothes. Robert looked up and stopped writing.

"Hey, Les, want to come out with me tonight?" Robert asked.

"Where to?" Lenard was a bit surprised that Robert was inviting him out, especially considering how mad he'd been about the mess Lenard had made and seeing that it was almost seven-thirty at night.

"To see a couple of women I know," Robert answered.

Lenard grew interested. "Anything in it for me?" he asked.

"Could be," Robert answered, then added quickly. "But these are ladies, Lenard. Put on your good clothes and wrap yourself up in your best manners!" Both men laughed. "You and I will grab some dinner at Jordan's first," Robert explained, "then we'll meet my girlfriend Virginia and her roommate later to go listen to some music."

"Have you asked them to meet us somewhere?" Lenard asked.

"No," Robert answered, "but they'll both be in tonight, and I can tap on their door or window and ask them to come with us to hear some music I know will be playing down in Storyville."

As Lenard changed his clothes, Robert removed his Colt .45 from the mantle. Lying beside the pistol were several bullets and a bullet mold. Robert loaded the gun and placed it in his overcoat pocket. At that moment, Lenard announced, "I'm ready!"

When Lenard saw that Robert had pocketed his pistol, Lenard took his .38 pocket revolver out of the nightstand drawer and stuck it in his pants' waistline, hiding it behind his jacket. The two men left their room to enjoy the evening.

After grabbing a bite at Jordan's, Robert and Lenard walked past Stendel's drugstore in the direction of Virginia's boarding house. As they passed, they saw a New Orleans' police officer sitting at the counter.

When they reached the house, Robert saw that Mrs. Cooley's upstairs light was on.

"Damn!" he said.

"What's the matter?" Lenard asked.

"The witch is still up," Robert answered, then explained. "That window belongs to the landlady. We can't go into the house until that upstairs light goes off."

“Maybe we should go back to Jordan’s or some other bar and come back later,” Lenard thought out loud.

Robert glanced at his pocket watch. “No,” he said. “She should be going to bed soon. Let’s wait.”

Lenard looked around and asked, “Where?”

Robert looked down the road in the direction of the drugstore, remembering the policeman inside. “We can’t go down to the drugstore with that policeman sitting there,” he said, looking in the other direction down the street. He nodded to his right and said, “Let’s sit on those steps over there.” Robert walked over to a house a few doors down from Virginia’s home. He had no idea that the house was where the white Schwartz family lived.

Nervous, Lenard said, “I don’t know about this, Robert. It don’t look right for two Negro men to be sittin’ ‘round in a mostly white neighborhood.”

Robert felt Lenard’s nervousness and had to admit to himself that there was an air of tension to the situation, but the thought of an evening out with Virginia went a long way to calming his nerves.

“Stay cool, Lenard,” Robert advised. “Everything’s okay. It’s a mixed neighborhood, and we won’t be here long.”

Robert sat down on the top step leading up to the house’s porch. Lenard sat next to Robert, but his right leg bounced up and down nervously. Lenard couldn’t stop fidgeting his hands either. Robert stayed perfectly still, but his face grew tense the more nervous Lenard became. He clasped his hands tightly together.

A white couple passed the men on the opposite side of the street and hurried into their home at the sight of Robert and Lenard sitting on the steps.

"Did you see the way they was looking at us?" Lenard asked Robert. "Let's get out of here, man!"

Robert placed a hand on Lenard's knee to stop it from bouncing. "Just sit tight, Les," Robert admonished. "You'll make them more nervous if you act so nervous yourself."

"Just seein' our black faces makes them nervous," Lenard said, "and that's makin' me nervous." Lenard stood up and said, "Come on."

Robert stayed seated where he was. When Robert didn't move, Lenard sat back down. A middle-aged white woman appeared on the front steps of the house next door. She said to Robert and Lenard, "You there! Who are you? What are you doing sitting on those steps?"

Robert remained calm and took off his hat, nodding his head to the neighbor, "Evening, ma'am. We're just waiting for a friend who lives a couple of doors down. We won't be long."

The woman did not seem satisfied. She stayed on her doorstep but called back through the front door she was holding ajar. "George!" she called out. "George! Come out here a minute!"

At that moment, the uniformed police officer walked out of Stendel's drugstore. The neighbor woman who had called for her husband saw the officer and rushed down her front steps just as George appeared.

"Where in tarnation are you going, Becky?" George yelled after his wife, a bit exasperated.

Becky waved at the policeman and met him about halfway between the drugstore and where Robert and Lenard sat. Robert watched cautiously as he saw the woman and police officer talking, the woman turning every once in a while to point to Robert and Lenard. Just as Robert stood up to leave, the police officer blew his whistle.

Moments later, Patrolmen Mora and Cantrelle appeared from around the corner. They quickly approached Robert and Lenard, who had sat themselves back down on the steps to appear less threatening. Mora tightly gripped the heavy wooden billet attached to his belt.

"What you boys doing sitting out here?" Mora asked Robert and Lenard.

Keeping his voice calm, Robert answered, "We're just waiting on a friend who lives a couple of houses down, officer."

"You should be waiting somewhere else," Mora stated. "You're frightening these people."

Robert tried to remain calm but let a hint of resentment seep through. He said, "They wouldn't be frightened if they would just mind their own business."

This statement, coming from a black man, triggered Mora's anger. Robert stood, and his height and broad shoulders alarmed Mora, who grabbed Robert's arm. Robert tried to pull his arm free, but Mora held tight. Being stronger, Robert pulled Mora into the street. Mora then pulled out his billet and started to hit Robert with it.

Robert jerked loose from Mora's grasp and ran. Mora pulled his gun and fired in Robert's direction. As he was running, Robert pulled out his Colt and returned Mora's fire. The men exchanged fire about three more times.

Robert stumbled and fell momentarily as a bullet grazed his left leg. He got up and ran off in a zigzag fashion down the darkening street, not knowing that one of his bullets had struck Mora in the right thigh while another had grazed his hand.

Cantrelle, who had stayed closer to the drugstore when Mora first approached Robert and Lenard, shot at Robert several times when he saw his partner fall. Robert had outdistanced the policemen by this time, and Cantrelle stopped firing to attend to Mora.

The police officer who had exited Stendel's first and blown his whistle, Sergeant Jules C. Aucoin, came running from the drugstore's relative safety. He now stood over Lenard with his gun aimed directly at the face of the frightened youth. Lenard clasped both hands together tightly behind his head. Having dashed for cover when the shooting started, George came back outside. He approached the policeman, whom he recognized as Sergeant Aucoin.

"You remember me?" George asked the Sergeant. "I'm George who has the lunch cart outside your station."

Although Sergeant Aucoin wasn't completely sure he recognized this man, he answered, "Of course."

"Has this man been searched?" George asked Aucoin.

Not waiting for an answer, George patted down a seated Lenard, feeling something under the young man's jacket. George reached behind Lenard's coat and pulled out a small .38 Webley Bull Dog pocket revolver stuck under his belt at the small of his back.

Cantrelle, bending over the bleeding Mora, looked up when he heard Sergeant Aucoin order, "Hand me that gun, sir. I don't want anyone else hurt."

George handed the sergeant Lenard's gun but didn't leave. Sergeant Aucoin, taking control of the situation, spoke over his shoulder at Cantrelle while he maintained his aim on the frightened Lenard.

"Officer Cantrelle," the sergeant commanded, "Get back to the drugstore and call for an ambulance. Now!"

Cantrelle jumped up and ran off in the direction of Stendel's. George's wife, who had instigated the confrontation, peeked out from behind the front door where she'd gone to hide when the shooting started. When she was sure the shooting had stopped, she ran down the steps to be with her husband.

"Becky," George said as she approached.

Becky didn't wait for her husband to say anything more before turning to the sergeant and saying, "There are two women who rent an apartment together in Mrs. Cooley's boarding house, two doors down. They're Negroes, but one of them does work at Charity Hospital. I don't think she's a nurse, but maybe she's an aide. She might know how to stop the bleeding or something."

Without hesitation, Sergeant Aucoin replied urgently, "Yes, go get them. And ask them to bring first-aid supplies. Tell them it's a serious gunshot wound. Go!"

Becky turned and started walking to Mrs. Cooley's house.

George shouted after his wife, telling her, "Hurry, woman!"

Becky picked up her pace and ran up Mrs. Cooley's front steps. She banged on the front door, shouting at the same time, "Charlotte! Charlotte, are you home? It's an emergency!"

Mrs. Charlotte Cooley, dressed for bed in her gown and housecoat, opened the front door. "Becky, whatever is the matter?" she asked her neighbor. "Did I hear shooting? Is George all right?"

"Oh, Charlotte," Becky answered quickly. "A policeman's been shot. Are your two tenants, the black girls, at home? One of them might be able to help."

Mrs. Cooley opened the front door and ushered Becky inside. "I think so. Come on in. We'll check."

Mrs. Cooley knocked loudly on Virginia's and Ernestine's apartment door, yelling, "Girls! Are you in? Virginia! Ernestine! We need your help! It's an emergency!"

Virginia opened her apartment door a crack. Both she and Ernestine had heard the shooting, but they had no idea what had happened, or to whom. When she saw it was Mrs. Cooley at the door, she opened it wide. Both Virginia and Ernestine still wore their work dresses.

"Mrs. Cooley!" Ernestine said with alarm. "What's going on? We heard shots!"

Becky didn't let Mrs. Cooley answer. She pushed her way in front of the landlady and spoke quickly to the women. "Girls! A policeman's been shot! Real bad in the leg. He's bleeding all over the place. I know one of you works at the hospital. Can you help him?"

Ernestine took a step back in surprise, and said to Becky, "I do work at Charity, but I'm not a nurse. I clean rooms."

"He's been shot in the leg and is bleeding everywhere," was Becky's only response to this news.

Virginia turned her back on the women and hurried to a cabinet in the small sitting room. She spoke loudly enough to be heard. "Ernestine, I still have that first aid kit we put together after our visit to the Negro nursing school at the medical college. Maybe we can at least help stop the bleeding."

Ernestine then addressed her landlady. "Go get us as many clean towels as possible, Mrs. Cooley."

Mrs. Cooley hesitated, whispering, "But my towels."

Ernestine cut Mrs. Cooley off. "Just go!" she demanded. "A man's life is at stake! He could bleed to death if a main vein or artery was hit."

Mrs. Cooley turned and ran up her stairs. Virginia returned from across the room carrying a beat-up leather satchel. She and Ernestine pushed their way past Becky and ran out the front door of the boarding house. Aucoin looked up and saw the two black women approach Mora. Becky was right behind and a few moments later Mrs. Cooley followed, carrying a stack of fresh towels.

When they got to the wounded man, Ernestine knelt to Mora's right and Virginia took up position to his left, opening the satchel.

Aucoin asked, "You two girls nurses?"

Ernestine, not wanting to waste time answering this man's questions, knew that his uniform could get in their way of helping his colleague so she replied authoritatively, "We're training to be nurses, and my ma was a midwife so I've learned first aid from the time I was a child." Her answer seemed to satisfy the sergeant.

Virginia took a pair of scissors out of the satchel and passed them handle-end up to Ernestine, who swiftly grabbed the scissors and cut Mora's blood-soaked pant leg from the cuff up. Virginia untied and removed Mora's boot from the foot of the wounded leg. She peeled off his sock. The entire leg was covered in blood.

Once the pant leg was out of the way, a large bullet wound was visible in his thigh. Ernestine grabbed a clean towel off the stack that Mrs. Cooley had placed on the sidewalk next to the wounded officer. With the towel folded, Ernestine pressed it with both hands firmly against the wound. Virginia took a thick, wide white cotton bandage roll out of her satchel. She unrolled it then doubled the cloth over twice to make it shorter and thicker. She slipped one end under Mora's hurt leg above the wound, and she tied the two ends very tightly to cut off the blood flow.

Ernestine looked over her shoulder to Becky and commanded, "Go boil a kettle of water in case we need it."

Without hesitation, Becky ran to her house next door.

The first towel Ernestine had pressed against Mora's leg wound was soaked through with blood. She tossed it aside and pressed a clean one against the injury. Mora moaned slightly with this new pressure on his wound, but it was clear that he was barely conscious.

She looked over at Virginia and asked, "Is there any antiseptic in the kit?"

"I remember putting in a bottle of hydrogen peroxide," Virginia answered, rummaging into the satchel to find the brown glass bottle. She pulled it out and asked Ernestine, "Do you want to use it on his leg?"

"No," her roommate answered. "It's more important to keep pressure on that wound right now. I noticed he had a bleeding injury on his hand. Pour the hydrogen peroxide over the wound. You'll see it bubble, but that means it's cleaning the wound. Then take some gauze and wrap his hand."

Virginia did exactly as she was instructed. While she was bandaging Mora's hand, Becky returned, walking carefully while carrying a large metal kettle with steam coming from its spout. She placed it on the ground beside Ernestine, who was keeping pressure on the leg wound. The tourniquet was working, however, so the second towel pressed against the bullet hole was not as bloody.

Ernestine took her hand off the towel against Mora's leg and grabbed the final two clean towels. She spread one open on the ground, and laid the other towel back down, still folded, on top of the open towel. She picked up the kettle and drenched the folded towel. She waited a moment, and when it wasn't too hot to pick up, she swapped the bloody towel on top of the bullet wound with the wet towel. She gently dabbed and wiped around the wound, cleaning it as best she could. When both the wound and the leg around it were cleared of blood, Ernestine told Virginia, "Give me any clean gauze and bandages left in the satchel."

Virginia handed her friend a brown unopened paper packet of gauze and the last cotton roll of bandaging. "There's also a jar of Vaseline® in the kit, Ernestine," she said.

Ernestine looked up with surprise and said, "Perfect! I can use it to keep the gauze and bandage from sticking to the wound."

After Virginia had passed her the glass jar of petroleum jelly, Ernestine used one clean wadding of gauze to smear the wound area with Vaseline®. She then stuffed the open hole in Mora's leg with more clean gauze. She finally wrapped the wound and leg with the cotton bandaging.

Cantrelle ran up from the drugstore. Ernestine didn't wait for him to speak. Looking at the open-faced watch she always wore pinned to her lapel, Ernestine asked, "How long ago did you call for the ambulance?"

Cantrelle took a small pocket watch from his top pant's pocket and looked at its face. "Just going on 25 minutes ago," he replied.

Ernestine creased her brow and said with concern in her voice, "If we want to save his leg, they'd better get here soon."

George demanded, “What dya‘ mean ‘save his leg’?”

Ernestine remained calm, refusing to be baited. “To keep him from bleeding to death, we had to cut off the flow of blood to the leg wound. He’d be dead now if we hadn’t done so.”

“What the…” George began.

Ernestine cut him off and continued. “If he can be taken into surgery in the next few hours, the surgeons can hopefully return the flow of blood to his leg to keep the tissue from dying. Any longer, and they’ll probably have to amputate his leg.”

At that moment a horse-drawn ambulance wagon pulled up alongside the women and their patient. Two men jumped down from the back of the wagon and pulled out a stretcher. They ran over to Mora. The stretcher bearer nearest Mora’s head, Ben, turned to Ernestine and Virginia while pulling out a small notebook and pencil from his pants’ pocket. He took notes while questioning them.

“What time was he shot, and how long has his leg been shut off?” he asked.

Ernestine answered efficiently, occasionally glancing at her pin watch. “He was shot approximately thirty-five minutes ago. We tied off his leg’s blood supply exactly twenty-two minutes ago so he bled for about seventeen minutes before we stemmed the flow.”

Ben finished jotting down what Ernestine had shared and put away the notebook and pencil. While Ben had been taking notes, Ted, the other stretcher bearer, enlisted George’s help to get Mora onto the stretcher.

Ben made sure Mora was properly positioned and directed Ted to cover Mora with a blanket up to his chin.

As he and Ted each took an end of the stretcher and lifted the policeman into the wagon, Ben said, "Excellent work, girls. No doubt you saved this man's life. I'll pass on this information to the doctors and nurses at Charity Hospital. Are you two nurses?"

Virginia answered, "No, not yet, but we've had first aid training."

Without acknowledging Virginia's answer, Ben took another look at Ernestine. "You look familiar," he said. "Have I seen you around the hospital?"

"I don't know," Ernestine said a bit abruptly. "Have you? I do work there."

A flash of recognition crossed Ben's face and he grinned. "That's right! I've seen you cleaning. I can't wait to tell Sister Josephine that a Negro janitress probably saved this man's life. She won't believe it," Ben laughed as he climbed into the back of the ambulance wagon to accompany the patient.

Ernestine and Virginia just stared after the departing wagon. Ernestine finally turned away and said to Virginia, "Let's get this area cleaned up."

While Virginia put the remaining supplies back in the satchel and picked up the trash, Ernestine wrapped the blood-soaked towels in the relatively clean towel she had spread out on the road. She stood while putting this bundle under her left arm. Mrs. Cooley was standing there.

Ernestine said to her, "Thank you for the towels, Mrs. Cooley," Ernestine said politely. "If you like, I'll take them with me to the hospital tomorrow and ask our laundry to sterilize and bleach them for you."

"Just throw them out, Ernestine," Mrs. Cooley answered with exasperation. "I couldn't bear to use them after…all this," she said, motioning to the blood-stained area.

Ernestine did not look directly at either Mrs. Cooley or the area where Mora had been lying. She said, "I can ask the hospital for some new, unused towels to replace these, if you'd like me to."

Not understanding the stress and trauma Ernestine and Virginia may have just experienced, Mrs. Cooley said, "Can you guarantee they're new and never been used by…" she hesitated then continued, "especially by colored…"

Ernestine cut off Mrs. Cooley, knowing what she was going to say. "Absolutely, Mrs. Cooley. I'll bring you an unopened, untouched, new, fully wrapped package of four towels. I won't even touch the towels myself."

"Very good, Ernestine," Mrs. Cooley said, turning and heading back to the house.

As the roommates finished clearing the area, Sergeant Aucoin walked Lenard down the few front stairs to the sidewalk while talking to George. He did not even acknowledge Virginia or Ernestine, the two women who had saved Mora's life.

"Thank you for your help, sir," Aucoin said to George. "Officer Cantrelle and I will take the prisoner from here."

Chapter 11

Nearing midnight, Monday, 23 July 1900, New Orleans

Robert hobbled down the narrow alley that ran beside his rooming house. His leg had bled slowly but steadily while he was running away from where he was shot, but by the time he reached the alley leading up to his ramshackle room, he wasn't leaving a trail. He had taken an unlikely route and backtracked to where he lived, taking his time to make sure he wasn't followed. He quietly entered his room without attracting attention. He was in survival mode. No time right now for figuring out what happened. Or why it happened. He wasn't even aware at this moment that he had tucked away the part of himself that worried about Lenard…and Virginia.

Inside a small enclosed room within the New Orlean's Sixth Precinct Stationhouse, Lenard sat in a straight-backed chair while Sergeant Aucoin stood with his back to the only door. The precinct's Captain John Day questioned Lenard.

"Now that you've got the lies out of your system, tell us the truth, Lenard," Captain Day demanded.

Aucoin, keeping his eyes on the prisoner, saw that Lenard was very frightened, too afraid to look directly at Day.

"I…I…swear to you, sir," Lenard stuttered, "we didn't mean no harm. I kept askin' to leave. I didn't want no trouble."

"You've got plenty of trouble on you now, boy," Day said. "So to get yourself out of it, tell me who was your friend? What's his name?"

Lenard looked down at his feet, hesitating. "We weren't real good friends. I just met him in a bar, and he said I should come with him to visit a couple of girls he knew."

"What girls?" Day asked.

"I don't know, sir," Lenard said, quick to be able to speak the truth. "I'd never done met 'em."

Captain Day turned to his Sergeant. "Aucoin, will you leave me alone with the prisoner? I think he'll talk better if there's just me to reckon with."

Sergeant Aucoin hesitated, but not wanting to be on the bad side of his boss, he answered, "Sure, Captain."

All three men knew full well what leaving Lenard alone with the Captain meant. As Aucoin turned to go, he heard Lenard plead, "Wait! Don't leave me here alone with him. I'll tell you what you want to know!"

"Hold on a minute, Aucoin," Day said. He turned back to Lenard. "Start talking, boy," the Captain commanded.

"His name's Robertson," Lenard said. "Curtis Robertson."

"Where does he live?" Day asked, believing that they were getting somewhere now.

"I don't know exactly, sir," Lenard said, with as much subservience as he could bring forth through the fear. “As I said, we just met in a bar, and most people in there called him Buster.”

“What bar?” Day asked.

“I think the name was Johnson’s or Johnny’s or somethin’ like that,” Lenard said, his nervousness showing through again.

“You met him just last night?” Day questioned.

“No…I mean…yes. I mean,” Lenard’s nerves and fear got the better of him as he hemmed and hawed. He finally blurted out, “I’ve seen him around, but just last night we got to talkin’.”

“And what did you talk about?” Day continued.

“Usual stuff. Girls mostly,” Lenard said. “That’s when he told me about the two girls we was goin’ to meet.”

Day’s questioning had been leading in one general direction, and with his next question he stepped firmly on the path he intended to take. “White women?” Day asked.

Aucoin could see that Lenard was visibly shocked by the question.

“No, sir!” he blurted out. “Absolutely no. They was Negro.”

“So you saw them?” Day asked, trying to trip up Lenard.

Although frightened and confused, Lenard stood firm on this point. “No, sir,” Lenard said with assurance. It was always easier for him when he spoke the truth, and his next words poured out. “Buster had told me he’d been seeing this pretty Negro woman and that she had a Negro roommate who I might like to meet.”

"So you did meet them," Day persisted.

"No, sir," Lenard insisted again. "Buster done tole me all this when we was eating supper."

"Now, Lenard," Captain Day went on, "Did this Buster Buck explain to you what two colored girls would be doing living in a white neighborhood?"

With his stomach in an even tighter knot, Lenard fell back on the truth. He said, "Robert, uh, I mean, Curtis…Buster…" Lenard stumbled, "he said they was nurses or wanted to be, and that some of them boarding houses in that neighborhood rented to whites and coloreds with jobs."

Sergeant Aucoin interrupted, speaking to his captain. "Captain, the two women who helped Mora were Negroes who knew a lot about first aid. Maybe they were the ones. They rent a room a couple of doors down from where the shooting took place. They rent from a white landlady, a Mrs. Cooley, if I remember correctly."

Without acknowledging what his sergeant had said, Day turned his attention back to Lenard. "Did you know there were white women in the house where you were sitting?"

In desperation, Lenard pleaded, "No, sir! I promise! Ya' gotta' believe me. Curtis just said he knew these two Negro girls and he wanted to take them to listen to some music. That's all I knows. I promise!"

Captain Day turned back to Aucoin. "Leave us, Sergeant!" he demanded.

Sergeant Aucoin, understanding his boss's tone, turned, opened the door, and left, all the while with Lenard pleading for him to stay.

Aucoin walked down the corridor leading from the interview room to the squad room, which was cramped and untidy. Several other officers worked at desks and talked among themselves, but everyone stopped what they were doing when Aucoin stepped into the room. He shook his head at his colleagues, and the men went back to what they were doing. A moment later they heard a heart-wrenching scream and crash from the interrogation room. The squad room went silent again.

Sergeant Aucoin tried to break the silence by speaking to a patrolman sitting at the desk across from his own. "I sure hope we get a lead on that maniac who shot Mora. Damn knows we don't want a wild beast like that roaming the streets of New Orleans or taking off to some other town."

The policeman agreed, "Yeah, he's probably out of the city by now. At least then it wouldn't be our problem."

A glance at his pocket watch told Robert that it was nearing two-thirty a.m.. He was still in his bedsit, which was lit by a single beat-up 1880s nickel-over-brass kerosene lamp. Other than the two beds, small desk, Robert's books, writing implements, clothes, and newspapers, there wasn't much else in this small room, certainly no water or medical supplies. Earlier, Robert had opened a few desk drawers until he found something he could use to treat his wound—a small glass jar of Vaseline® and some green gauze.

Now, with his leg still throbbing, Robert limped over to the corner of the room for his Winchester rifle. He took a bag of ammunition out of his desk drawer and sat back down on the bed to load the rifle. He put his remaining supply of .22 Long cartridges, the bullet mold, a few short-lengths of lead and steel pipes, and his new blue suit into his leather satchel.

Robert reached under his bed and pulled out a small metal box, the one his brother Henry had mailed him when he first moved to New Orleans. Robert opened it and took out what cash he had. He glanced around the room to see if there was anything else he wanted to take with him before leaving the room that had been his home the past couple of months. He had lived in a number of different rooms during his six years in New Orleans, but he had a way of making each place he lived feel a little bit like a home, given his books, journals, newspapers, and other paraphernalia of his life's interests.

He saw his most recent composition book sitting on top of the desk. When he thought about his years of journaling, Robert's heart sank. 'That's my life," he said to himself. He just couldn't see walking away from all that had been part of who he was as a person. His books. His piece of African art, even if broken. His writings. His hopes.

The part of himself that wanted to survive shouted out to him, "Robert. Don't be a fool. Staying alive is what matters!"

"But I have a life here!" Robert argued with himself, however impossible he knew that argument to be.

"If you stay here or weigh yourself down with these pieces of your past, your life will be dangling from the end of a rope by sun up." This logic won the argument.

Outside the Sixth Street Stationhouse, Patrolman Cantrelle and several other policemen pulled up in a horse-drawn patrol wagon. Just as Cantrelle was getting out of the wagon, Captain Day came rushing out of the station house.

"Any luck, Cantrelle?" Day asked.

"No, sir," Cantrelle answered. "We followed the bloodstains as best we could, but there weren't a lot of them. And it looks like he backtracked quite a bit. Seems like he's a smart devil."

Dismissing Cantrelle's claim of Robert's intelligence, Day said, "He's just showing the instincts of a hunted animal. Come on, I got his address from the boy. And his name is Robert Charles, not Curtis Robertson. Or Buster."

Lenard lay curled on his left side, his face and torso bruised and cut. His blood stained the floor beneath the bare metal cot. Both eyes were swollen shut, and Lenard could barely breathe through his mouth, let alone his nostrils. His broken nose was caked with clotted blood. His right shoulder felt dislocated, and at least five ribs were broken. Captain Day had pummeled Lenard's abdomen while wearing a heavy metal and onyx ring on the fourth finger of his right hand. The blood that dripped from Lenard's worst gash on his belly joined the remains of Lenard's dinner that he vomited up when first thrown into the holding cell. Without really knowing it, Lenard was given some grace as he passed out from the pain.

Around 3:00 a.m., Tuesday, 24 July 1900, New Orleans

A patrol wagon halted a block away from the establishment that housed Robert's one-room apartment. Captain Day and his six officers—Corporals Honore Perrier and Ernest Trenchard, Patrolmen Caspar Pincon, Peter Lamb and Joseph Cantrelle, who had encountered Robert Charles initially, and Sergeant Aucoin—jumped off the wagon and walked toward the alleyway they had been told led to Robert's bedsit. Two white civilians, Schmidt and Wallace, joined the group as it approached the head of the alley.

The larger of these two men, Wallace, spoke to Day. "You best be careful of him," Wallace warned the captain.

"He's probably not here anyway," Day scoffed, "and if he is, I can handle the nigger myself."

At that statement, Day pulled Lenard Pierce's .38 out of his pocket. It was better than his own service-issued revolver so he had brought it with him instead. As he readied himself, Captain Day issued orders to his officers.

"Cantrelle, Pincon, and Perrier—you scatter along the street and keep your eyes open."

"Yes, sir," Cantrelle answered for the three.

Day continued. "Aucoin, bring Trenchard and Lamb and come with me."

Wallace didn't make a move to join the group, but his friend, Schmidt, stepped forward and told Day he had been in the army and volunteered to go with the policemen. This contingent of five men, lit by three hand-held lanterns, headed for the entrance to the alley.

Just as Robert was about to leave his room he heard noises and saw the flash of lanterns just down the alley outside his window. He had already extinguished his lamp so he was in the dark. He limped quietly to his door. Robert quietly set his leather satchel on the floor next to him and made sure his Colt, which was tucked into his belt, was accessible. Robert held the Winchester poised, waiting and listening through a crack in the door.

Day entered the alley first, holding the pistol ahead of him, followed by Aucoin. Trenchard, Lamb, and Schmidt—each carrying a lantern—followed their Captain and Sergeant. Day knocked on the door to room

No. 1 where Fanny Jackson, a middle-aged black woman, lived and was sleeping. After a few moments a sleepy Miss Jackson opened her door a crack.

Day demanded, "Tell me where Robert Charles and Lenard Pierce live."

Fanny, scared and hesitant, asked, "What's the matter? Is…is he in trouble?"

Day hissed, "If you don't want any trouble, just tell me!"

Fanny said quietly, "Fourth door down," and pointed to her right. She quickly closed her door and retreated into the dark of her room.

The small alley's muddy passage was lined with wooden planks, which creaked and moaned as the men made their way down to Room No. 4. Barely ten feet away from Robert's door, Captain Day stopped, keeping his pistol raised in front of him.

Behind him, Corporal Trenchard shouted unexpectedly while holding his lantern above him, "Open up, Charles! It's the police!"

Robert's door opened suddenly. In the glow of the lantern light, Robert stood staring straight at Captain Day. Robert aimed his rifle directly at Day, who stood frozen in surprise. Robert used that moment to pull the trigger. This time he didn't avert his aim. Robert shot the lead policeman directly in the heart. Blood drenched the front of Day's uniform and he dropped Lenard's pistol just as he gave a small gasp of surprise and fell dead in the alleyway.

For about two seconds everyone, including Robert, stood still. Schmidt, at the back of the group, dropped his lantern, turned, and ran out of the alley. Aucoin shouted to Trenchard and Lamb, "Put out your lights!" Trenchard's lantern extinguished as he dropped it. Lamb turned off the lantern and joined Aucoin and Trenchard as they all three threw themselves against the wall of the alleyway across from Robert's room. They were very startled at the unexpected shooting—so much so they didn't realize they weren't out of Robert's firing line. Robert fired one more shot into Day's body…just to make sure he was dead. The policemen stared in disbelief at their Captain's body.

Taking advantage of this small opportunity, Robert stepped back into his room, pressing himself against the wall to the side of the open door as he reloaded his rifle. He shouted with rage as he did so, "I will not let you kill me. I'm going to kill you all!"

Robert stepped back into the doorway, his rifle raised, and aimed at the men lined up across from him. He fired. A bullet entered Patrolman Lamb's right eye, blowing apart his face. Aucoin, as if coming out of a trance, raised his pistol and fired two shots in Robert's direction, missing him entirely.

Trenchard, his pistol raised but his right hand shaking badly, attempted to shoot but his pistol malfunctioned. The sound of another shot caused Trenchard to drop his weapon. Both Aucoin and Trenchard, backed up against the wall opposite of Robert and stood as if frozen.

Seeing no guns pointed at him, Robert slammed his door shut. The door to No. 2, two rooms down from Robert, opened slightly. Annie Cryder, a middle-aged

Creole woman, looked out the door toward Trenchard and Aucoin. She shouted, "Come in here, you two!" The two frightened officers shuffled quickly to Annie's open door. They barely made it inside her room.

Robert heard Annie's shout, and with a small glimpse out his small front window, Robert saw the policemen trying to escape. Robert opened his door, stepped into the alley with his rifle raised, and aimed at Annie's room just as she slammed her door shut.

Annie guided the officers to an open closet in her room, blowing out her room's lamp as she passed it. The three remained quiet just inside the closet listening for sounds from the alley. They heard Robert shouting, "Come on out, you goddamn hound dogs. I dare you! Send them out, Annie! I don't want to hurt you!"

Robert was the only person in the alley. He stood with his rifle aimed at the small window of Annie's bedsit. All was quiet with no sign of movement in her room. After a moment, Robert walked slowly and carefully to the end of the alley from which the officers had entered. He kept his rifle held directly in front of him as he approached the alley's entrance.

Following the Captain's earlier orders, Office Pincon stood on a street corner at the opposite end of the block, quite a distance away. Perrier and Cantrelle stood under a street lamp about 75 yards away, Cantrelle facing the alley as Perrier looked nervously up and down the main street. They had heard the shots but figured a group of four armed men had done their duty and shot the animal dead. It was too dark for them to see Robert in the alley's entranceway.

Robert aimed his rifle at the two officers under the streetlamp and fired, his bullet grazing Perrier's hat and knocking it off his head. Perrier and Cantrelle automatically turned away from the alley and ran for their lives. Robert reentered the alley and disappeared.

Further down the road, Pincon didn't know what was happening and his only thought was to make it back to the police wagon, not easy to accomplish since Perrier had handed off their only lantern.

At that moment, the police wagon pulled up next to Pincon on the street corner, and he scrambled into the passenger seat, accepting the driver's proffered hand. Barely giving Pincon time to sit, the driver raised his whip. The horses pulled the wagon into motion, encouraged by the lashes to gallop as fast as they could past the alley's entrance. The driver and Pincon heard a rifle shot as they passed, the bullet whizzing behind them as they bolted down the road.

Robert reappeared in the alley entrance, carefully looking in both directions with his rifle raised. When he saw that all police presence was gone, Robert stepped back into the darkened alley. Just under ten minutes later, he reappeared in the entrance and stepped carefully into the main street once he saw it was still clear. He moved cautiously with his back to the stores making sure he could see up and down the street as he made his escape. He carried his leather satchel over his shoulder, his Colt was in his pocket, and the Winchester in his arms, poised to shoot if necessary. He was wearing his new suit.

Before Dawn, Tuesday, 24 July 1900, New Orleans

As the daylight brought shadows into Annie's single room, Trenchard and Aucoin approached the front door cautiously, not certain if the shooter was still in the area. They cracked the door and looked up and down the alley. There were no sounds and no sign of Robert Charles.

Aucoin, with tiredness in his voice, turned to look at Annie and said, "You saved our lives, Miss Cryder. That was a mighty brave thing to do."

Annie responded without much enthusiasm, "I'd do the same for anybody, Officer Aucoin."

Aucoin nodded in understanding and said, "Still, I do thank you."

The light in the alley was faint at best. Making sure the alley still was empty in both directions, the two policemen timidly stepped into it. Aucoin began to check on the fallen bodies of his comrades-in-arms. At the last moment, he thought better of it, turned, and he and Trenchard dashed to the alleyway entrance.

Life along the street picked up as the new day presented itself. A few men unlocked the doors to their street-front shops. A couple of horse-drawn wagons moved up and down the street, and one or two boys rode by on bicycles.

Entering the street, Trenchard and Aucoin took off running in the direction of the station. A few men gathered on the sidewalk a couple of doors down from the alley tried to stop them as they ran past, but they kept running until they made it to the police station, where the other officers began questioning Aucoin and Trenchard. The fact that Trenchard never fired his weapon, dropped it, and ran for cover led his colleagues and superiors to accuse him of cowardice.

Chapter 12

Early Morning, Tuesday, 24 July 1900, New Orleans

The telephone in the entranceway to the home of New Orleans' Superintendent of Police Dexter Gaster rang shrilly, awakening Gaster, his wife, and their daughters. Gaster came down the hallway stairs, his left hand on the banister and his right hand passing over his still-sleepy face. As the high-pitched ringing continued, Gaster reached the phone and lifted the receiver to his ear.

"Hello," Gaster answered, sounding groggy and disoriented. He listened for a moment, then grumbled, "What?" Gaster listened again, clearing the sleep out of his throat. He stood up straighter with increasing awareness and alarm at what he was hearing.

"What did you say?" he asked again. "Just a minute." Gaster pulled the receiver away from his ear and shouted up the stairs, where his wife, Julie, leaned over the railing.

"Jules," he said, "get my uniform out and put it on the bed. And please hurry!"

Julie didn't hesitate.

Back on the phone, Gaster stated, "Okay. Give me the details. Uh-huh…Uh-huh…Who? Day? And Lamb? Oh, sweet Jesus!…What? Mora? Is he okay?…Uh-huh…Okay. I'll be on my way in fifteen minutes. I should be there in thirty. Hold down the fort until I get there."

Gaster slammed the phone's earpiece down so quickly that he missed and the receiver was left hanging off the side table as he dashed up the stairs two steps at a time.

His two teenage daughters met him at the top of the stairs. Gaster looked at them both and pointed his finger at one girl and then the other while saying, "Now you girls, listen to me! You stay INSIDE all day today, you hear me! And tell your mother to do the same. Don't you dare go out for ANYTHING. I'll explain later."

Not giving either his daughters or his wife, who was back on the landing, a chance to ask any questions, Gaster pushed past them and entered his bedroom, slamming the door behind him. His family just looked at each other before Julie shuffled her daughters into the girls' bedroom.

As reporters arrived for work at the *Daily States*, Major Hearsey sat in his glass-walled office sorting through the papers on his desk. Billings came striding through the bullpen's main door, announcing to everyone, "Have you heard about the shooting?"

O'Malley, already at his desk, didn't look up but stopped typing. "What shooting?" he asked.

Billings came over to O'Malley's desk and said, "Someone killed two policemen and wounded another one last night. There's a manhunt going on for the shooter, and I hear there may be more trouble."

O'Malley looked up at Billings as the rest of the bullpen grew quiet. The reporter closest to Major Hearsey's office knocked on the editor's door and didn't wait for an invitation to open it. "I think you better hear this, sir," he said to Hearsey.

Hearsey looked up, stood, and walked around his desk, pushing the reporter aside as he stepped into the bullpen. He saw Billings standing at O'Malley's desk but talking to the entire room. Hearsey pushed his way to the center of the bullpen, where he asked loudly and with authority, "Billings, what's that you're saying?"

"There's not much to tell at this point, sir," Billings said. "On my way in this morning I heard that a man shot and killed two New Orleans policemen. That's about it so far."

"Do they have the shooter?" Hearsey demanded.

"No, sir," Billings answered. "The gunman's still at large, and I haven't heard anything about who he is."

Hearsey turned to O'Malley and asked, "Don't you know anything about it, O'Malley? Police is your beat."

"This is the first I've heard of it," O'Malley said, quick to explain. "I've been here most of the night, sir, working on a story. I was to meet my police contacts in thirty minutes to get the scoop on anything that happened overnight." O'Malley stood up from his desk, gathered a few papers, stuffed them in his attaché case, and said, "But I'll get on it right away."

"You do that," Hearsey bellowed. "Get the names of the dead officers first and phone them in to Billings. I want it on page one in this afternoon's two-thirty edition."

O'Malley left the bullpen quickly, glancing at Billings on his way out. The senior reporter raised his eyebrows, wondering just what the day might bring.

Morning, Tuesday, 24 July 1900, New Orleans

Gaster, in full uniform, arrived at the intersection of Robert's alley and the main street. He stepped out from the back seat of a new Oldsmobile driven by an officer in uniform. Gaster worked his way through a growing crowd to reach the roped-off alley entrance. O'Malley reached the entrance just as Gaster did.

O'Malley spoke to a police officer standing guard. "I'm with the *Daily States*," he said. "Can I get in?"

The policeman hesitated then, seeing Gaster, said, "Hang on a minute. The Chief hasn't been in yet." The policeman held the rope down for Gaster as the superintendent stepped over it. O'Malley tried to follow, but another officer stopped him.

As Gaster made it down to the part of the alleyway where the action occurred, four policemen were in the process of removing the bodies of Day and Lamb. Another patrolman stood guard outside Robert's door. Gaster addressed this policeman. "Open up the door for me, officer."

The patrolman swung the door open and stepped aside for Gaster to enter. A moment later Gaster came back out, shouting up to the alley entrance. "Richards," Gaster yelled, "get Williams and Brown to search this room. I want them to look for anything that might tell us where this man may be headed."

Gaster followed the men carrying the bodies of Day and Lamb on stretchers back up to the alley entrance. Other reporters gathered here along with O'Malley. They stopped Gaster with their rapid-fire questions. O'Malley made himself heard over the other reporters.

"Superintendent Gaster," he shouted. "Can you tell us the names of the officers who were killed? And the ones wounded?"

Gaster turned to Sergeant Richards, who was helping keep the crowd back, and asked him, "Richards, have their families been notified?"

"Yes, sir," Richards answered. "Garvey sent a chaplain with the news to each of the families about two hours ago."

Gaster turned back to the reporters. "The officers who were gunned down and killed early this morning were Captain John Day and Patrolman Peter Lamb," Superintendent Gaster stated. "You can get information about their excellent service records at the Sixth Precinct. Only one officer was wounded. Patrolman August Mora was shot on Monday evening at another location. He's currently at Charity Hospital. It was the same shooter in both instances."

"Who did this?" O'Malley questioned, taking notes as fast as information was thrown at him.

"All indications point to a Negro man name of Charles, Robert Charles," Gaster confirmed. "I can tell you right now. I want him, and I want him now!"

Other reporters tried to break in with questions, but Gaster wouldn't let them. "When my men find him," he said with all the authority of his position, "they have orders to shoot on sight if he offers any resistance. Now, if you'll excuse me, I have to get downtown. Sergeant Richards can fill you in on the details." Gaster worked his way back to the waiting Olds.

The reporters pushed in closer to Richards, who just managed to send Inspectors Williams and Brown down to search Roberts' room before he was inundated by the city's reporters.

Mid-Morning, Tuesday, 24 July 1900, New Orleans

Robert had arrived at the small duplex home of Silas and Martha Jackson before dawn broke. Silas had already left for work, and Robert had found Martha cleaning up the early morning breakfast dishes.

Now the two of them sat in Martha's and Silas's upstairs bedroom, which was beside the duplex bedroom two of their adult children shared. Robert jumped up to look out the window every few minutes. Clearly nervous herself, Martha tried to calm Robert.

"Just sit down, Robert," she said. "We can't think if you're jumping up every minute."

Robert sat back down and said, "It's just for a day…two at the most. Until my leg stops hurting so badly, and I can walk on it better."

Martha spoke gently to Robert. “I know I promised your mama that I’d keep an eye on you, but I wasn’t expecting you to get in this kind of trouble.”

Robert, sitting on the bed next to Martha, covered her hand with his to stop it from shaking. Keeping his voice as calm as possible, Robert said, “I know, Martha. And neither was I. You’ve been a good friend. You and Silas both. Believe me. It’s nothing to get too worried about. I just had a scrape with the police. I can be out of here no later than the day after tomorrow.”

Martha thought for a moment then said to Robert, “We’re renting the downstairs room out to Burke, but he’s gone for a couple of days. There’s a closet under the stairs. You can hide in it, but we’ll have to talk to Silas when he gets home.”

Robert smiled weakly at Martha and said, “Sure. That’s fine. And thank you, Martha.” Robert got up and looked out the window again.

Noticing that Robert’s limp was worse, Martha told him, “You better lie down and rest. Let me tend to that leg.”

Back at Robert’s house, a bloodhound, Sinclair, tugged at his leash, anxious to follow the scent. His dog handler, Robbie, held tight to the leash, commanding Sinclair to stay put.

Inspector Williams, in charge of the scene, handed one more piece of Robert’s clothing to Robbie. “Have the dog sniff this shirt,” he said.

Sinclair took in all the scents the shirt had to offer and howled.

"He's ready to roll, Inspector," Robbie announced, just as Sinclair nearly pulled his handler off his feet and started following the trail down the alley in the opposite direction of the main street. Sinclair and Robbie made it almost to the opposite end of the alley when Sinclair stopped and bayed at a shed-like outbuilding.

Robbie shouted down the alley in the direction of Robert's room. "Hey, Richards," he yelled. "We got something down here."

Richards and two other officers ran to the shed. Sinclair pawed frantically at the door, which Richards approached and listened through before opening it. "It's empty," he said, directing one of the other policemen to open the door.

Stepping inside the opened shed, Richards found a pile of clothes lying on the floor. Richards held up the pants, stained with blood, and handed them to Robbie. "How 'bout these?" he asked.

Robbie, trying to control Sinclair, responded, "Perfect. This blood will give Sinclair here a stronger scent to follow."

What both men didn't know was that Robert, after stripping down to nothing inside the shed, stepped naked across the alley to a rain barrel and washed his body of all traces of blood, except for the bit that bled through his leg's make-shift bandage. He redressed in the blue pinstripe suit he'd just bought, a suit he'd never worn before, presuming the police would be sending dogs after him.

Robbie took the pants from Richards and held them out for Sinclair to sniff, saying, "Thatta boy. Okay. Let's find the bastard!" As Sinclair and his handler headed back to the alley entrance, with Sinclair pulling hard at his leash, it began to rain, a slow patter at first. Sinclair stopped at the entrance and whimpered. A group of reporters still gathered at the alley entrance held back by a few uniformed officers.

Robbie leaned down to pet Sinclair while telling Richards, "Damn! This rain's gonna put a damper on old Sinclair's nose here."

Irritated, frustrated, and borderline angry, Richards yelled, "It's just startin' to rain. Keep that dog movin'!"

Robbie, petting Sinclair, said, "We'll do our best, but if the rain picks up, ain't nothin' we can do about it." Robbie held out Robert's bloodstained pants for Sinclair to take another sniff. "Come on, boy," he coaxed Sinclair. "Keep'a goin' best you can."

Sinclair led Robbie a bit farther down the sidewalk and along the street on which Robert had fled. The rain went from a drizzle to a downpour in a matter of a few minutes, and soon Sinclair stopped pulling at his leash and looked up at his handler with an expression that asked, "Have I disappointed you?"

Richards stood at the alley's entrance looking down the street at Sinclair and his handler, and said, "Shit!" as the rain came down harder. A door slammed, taking Richards' attention away from the dead-end dog. Inspectors Williams and Brown, finished in Roberts' room, walked back up the alley. Brown held a small wooden crate about half filled with papers. He'd thrown his police jacket over the top, trying to keep the papers dry in the rain.

Williams shouted as he walked toward Richards, "We're all through. We've got a bunch of stuff, and it looks pretty interesting."

Richards held up his hand, trying to quiet Williams. He nodded slightly to the group of reporters still gathered at the alley entrance. "Okay, Inspectors," Richards said a bit louder than necessary. "Get your report to Gaster right away."

As Williams and Brown walked swiftly up the street, a couple of reporters broke from the group and followed them. The rest of the reporters, including O'Malley, pushed closer to Richards.

"Okay, boys," Richards told the reporters, "it's all yours."

He stood aside as the reporters, with O'Malley leading the group, rushed into the alley. After Gaster had announced the names of the dead policemen, O'Malley found a phone and called the names into Billings as instructed. He had just made it back to the alleyway entrance in time to be given a shot at Robert's room.

The room was in complete disarray, with books thrown all about. Most of the books had torn-out pages and broken spines. Newspapers and leaflets littered the floor. A couple of younger reporters started picking them up.

Marcus Reed, with barely six months of on-the-job experience, scanned the newspaper he was holding. "Hey, look at this," he shared with his competitors. "This guy must've been a real troublemaker."

Larry Jones, with only a couple years' more experience, asked Marcus, "Why's that?"

"All these are incendiary papers and fliers about Negroes voting and demanding other rights." Marcus explained.

O'Malley barely listened to Marcus's gibberish. Robert's library intrigued Thomas. He checked each book's title as he picked it up, carefully making note of the more interesting books, some of them clearly school textbooks. As he reached for a book he spotted under Robert's bed, his hand hit something hard. He felt a small trunk that Williams and Brown clearly had missed. O'Malley went back to making notes, hoping the other reporters would soon grow bored and leave.

A *Picayune* reporter, Lucas Townsberry, dashed into the bedroom out of breath. "They just found his girlfriend," Lucas shouted, "She's with the Super at headquarters."

That statement decided it for Marcus. He told the others, "Well, I've seen about all I need to here. A girlfriend might prove interesting."

"Yeah," Larry agreed, dropping the newspapers and leaflets he was holding onto one of the beds. "Besides. I'm sure the police took out everything that might help find this guy."

Marcus, Larry, and Lucas, followed by the other few reporters left in Robert's room, headed out the door. The last one called over his shoulder, "You coming, O'Malley?"

O'Malley replied enthusiastically, to keep the others from coming back into the room, "I'll catch up with you in just a minute. Nature calls!"

Once he was sure the other reporters were on their way to headquarters, O'Malley pulled the trunk out from under Robert's bed and carefully opened it. Stacks of composition books filled the trunk, not what Thomas was expecting.

Thomas flipped through one of the top notebooks and saw that it was filled with neat cursive handwriting. Robert Charles's name was written on the front inside cover. O'Malley read what was written on page one:

> *Thursday, 31 May 1900*
> *Today's Picayune*[20] *had a headline story about the British marching into Pretoria, South Africa. The Boers abandoned the city and now the imperialists are going to take control. The British Empire...all they want are the gold and diamonds in southern Africa. Even the Dutch and French didn't care much for the native Africans. I can only imagine what this city was like before whites took control. One of my books on the history of Africa said that this part of the great continent was home to the Ndebele people. They may have been related to the Zulus. I did*

read that there were great initiation rites when children become adults.

I wonder what those ceremonies were like? Did all the families gather? Was there a great celebration? I can only imagine there was, for what more important passage is there other than from child to adult...when each of us becomes responsible for ourselves and others? When we become adults it is our time to step into the world as a doer...as a person who can act, to build a life. We marry and have families as adults. We work to earn our keep, making a home for our families, just like Mama and Pa did. We become part of a larger society. Going to church. Sending our children to school. Taking part in government. As adults we shape our world. What better time to celebrate than when becoming an adult?

O'Malley stood still for a moment, a torrent of questions flooding his mind. But two questions rose to the surface. Who was this man, and why had he killed two policemen? He knew the puzzle was much more complex than these two simple queries, but a journalist had to start somewhere. He sensed that most of the answers would be in these journals.

Thomas sat on the floor next to the trunk and started going through the composition books with fascination.

He discovered notes on a variety of topics, most of which were inspired by what Robert had read in either newspapers or books. Rarely did this most interesting man expound on his daily life—what happened at work, the gossip around the neighborhood, or what pretty girl had grabbed his attention. What did strike O'Malley was the wealth of insight and emotions—especially when writing about the injustices whites violently hurled upon Negroes to keep them oppressed—that evolved into ideas for solutions.

Realizing that he couldn't read all the journals here, O'Malley stuffed a small stack of composition books into his thin attaché. Only four of the thickish books fit in the already full case. "Damn it all!" O'Malley cursed.

He unbuttoned the top few shirt buttons and stuck four more journals between his shirt and undershirt. He picked up four more notebooks and stuffed them between his belted pants and waist. Thomas used his foot to close the trunk and push it back under Robert's bed, figuring he could come back for the rest. O'Malley looked carefully around the entire room, knowing that he was still a long way from understanding this man, Robert Charles.

As O'Malley stepped outside Robert's room, an alarming-sized crowd of people—men, women, children, blacks, and whites—had gathered in the alley. A short way from the crowd at Robert's door, a group of white men huddled together. A somewhat older man dressed in merchant seaman garb, Ed McCarthy, spoke to a couple of men closest to him.

"He could've been defending himself," McCarthy argued, "and in any case, he 'should be given a fair show.'[21] We don't know everything yet."

The man to his right, Hector, jabbed his index finger into McCarthy's upper chest and spoke harshly with emotion. "We know all we need to know!" Hector declared. "He shot and killed two policemen. Don't no one shoot at policemen 'less he's done some'um wrong!"

His buddy, Clement, joined Hector's argument. "That's right, Hector. Besides, he's a nigger! Any nigger who kills a white man, especially two policemen, don't deserve no fair show."

Ed McCarthy grew angry at this statement. "That proves my point. They might have shot at him first just because he's a Negro," he pointed out hotly.

Clement leaned in to McCarthy and asked rudely, "You a Yankee?"

McCarthy, putting his fists on his hips and looking directly at Clement, challenged him, "So what if I am? Want to make something of it?"

Hector stepped directly up to the tall seaman and yelled, "I'll make some'um of it all right! You ain't nothin' but a nigger-lovin' some-of-a-bitch Yankee traitor! We string up rats like you down here!"

The crowd of white men around McCarthy picked up Hector's cry, shouting and pumping their fists in the air. "Lynch him! Lynch the Yankee. Lynch the nigger-lovin' son-of-a bitch!" they cried.

Two uniformed police officers stationed in the alley to help control the crowd pushed through the circle of shouting white men. They each grabbed one of McCarthy's arms and pulled him through the angry crowd, rescuing him. Once they had him out of danger, Patrolman Gregg held on to McCarthy's arm, speaking directly at the man he considered to be a rabble rouser.

"You're coming with us down to the station," Gregg told McCarthy.

Slightly alarmed and a bit defiantly, McCarthy shouted, "What? Why's that? What in the hell did I do?"

Gregg responded with more authority and a bit louder, "We're going to have to charge you with making incendiary remarks and disturbing the peace."

Members of the crowd's outer ring heard this statement and cheered. The police turned and quickly led McCarthy to the alley entrance, away from the crowd.

Afternoon, Tuesday, 24 July 1900, New Orleans

Down at police headquarters, Superintendent Gaster sat behind his desk, and Virginia Banks sat nervously across from him in a straight-backed chair. The door to Gaster's office was closed, and a uniformed police officer stood at attention with his back to the door.

Gaster spoke to Virginia with authority. "I hope you appreciate the situation you're in, Miss Banks," he said. "Now I know you helped Patrolman Mora a great deal. I heard the surgeons were able to save his leg. But if you know where Mr. Charles is, you must tell us. Otherwise, you'd be aiding and abetting a criminal guilty of a capital crime, and that's a serious felony in and of itself."

Virginia, slightly nervous, but with enough show of courage to keep Gaster off balance, said, "Yes, Superintendent Gaster. I know what serious trouble this is, and I would not commit a crime for any reason…or for anybody. But when I helped that policeman I didn't even know Robert Charles had been around. I don't see him that often."

Shocked and somewhat stunned at this reply, Gaster said, "Miss Banks, it's clear you don't know what serious trouble you're in. Two distinguished police officers are dead and another one is in the hospital with a serious wound." Gaster leaned forward and pointed his finger directly at Virginia. "Tell me right now, Miss Banks," he demanded, "has Mr. Charles been in touch with you and, if he has, tell me where he is!"

All Virginia's bravado left her, and she answered nervously, "Sir, I don't know where Robert Charles is or even where he lives."

Gaster eased up on Virginia. "But according to his friend, Lenard Pierce, he and Robert were waiting for you and your roommate last night a few houses down from yours."

"Superintendent Gaster, I promise you," Virginia implored. "I had no idea Robert and his friend were out there. Ernestine and I were in our rooms after work. We had no plans to go out that evening. I tell you, I had no idea Robert and his friend had come to see us. We did hear shooting, but we had no idea what it was about. Even when my neighbor and our landlady told us a policeman had been shot, I didn't know that Robert was involved. I swear!"

Believing his harsher tone got better results, Gaster again threatened Virginia. "Miss Banks, all it would take is one word from me and that policeman standing outside my door could arrest you as a material witness in this case. Have you ever spent a night in jail? I can guarantee that you will spend a lot more than one night in jail if you don't start giving me some answers that mean something. Do you understand?"

Virginia clutched her hands together and was close to tears. "Yes, sir," she began. "It's just…it's just that…I'm frightened."

Gaster, taking the calmer tack again, said, "I didn't mean to frighten you, Miss Banks. I just want you to understand how serious this situation is. There's no need to be so scared that you can't talk to me."

Virginia, knowing just how serious the situation was becoming, knew she had to distance herself from Robert. She dropped her hands into her lap and took a deep breath before saying, "It's not that, sir. I'm frightened of Robert. It's true that I've known Robert for a few years. We met at a social club we both belong to, and he took an interest in me for some reason. I was not interested in him, but he persisted, and we did go out a couple of times, the last time about six months ago. The only reason I kept going out with him was because he scared me. He is a thug, sir. He has beaten me at times, and I'm awfully scared of him. That's why I hadn't seen him for so long until the other night when I accidentally ran into him at a meeting. I didn't want to see him, but like I say, I was scared, so I went along with him."

"Meeting?" Gaster demanded. "What meeting?"

This question startled Virginia. Thinking quickly, she replied, "Uh, no, sir. It was a dance. At the social club where we originally met."

Gaster waited, then he asked, "So did you spend time with Robert Charles, Miss Banks?"

Virginia paused for a moment, thinking how to get out of the hole she was digging for Robert...and herself. She took another deep breath and sat up a little straighter, looking directly at Gaster. With a bit more confidence in her voice, Virginia said, "Robert Charles scared me and said if I didn't go out with him again...Sir, I escaped him many times, but he always found me and beat me up for having run away from him."[17] Virginia paused and continued, "This time he said he had plans..."

Gaster, surprised, asked, "Plans? What kind of plans?"

"He had been talking about migrating to Africa," Virginia answered quickly. "He wanted to get together to tell me about that."

Gaster hesitated before saying, "I need information that will help me. I don't give two hoots what Mr. Charles planned to do. I want to hold him accountable for what he's already done. Tell me where I can find him."

"I tell you, sir," Virginia stated. "I have no idea..."

A knock on the door interrupted Virginia. Inspector Williams stepped into the office. Gaster, irritated at being interrupted, asked, "What is it, Williams?"

"Sir," Williams began, "Brown and I finished going through the papers we found in the suspect's room, and I've typed up a report."

Williams stepped toward Gaster's desk and handed over several typed sheets of paper. Gaster took them from Williams, saying dismissively while scanning the report's top page, "Thank you, Williams. I'll be with you in a moment."

Williams nodded at his superior, turned, and walked out of the office. Gaster placed the report in front of him on his desk. He saw Virginia looking at him and then at the desk. Gaster quickly turned the report typed-side down. He put his hands, fingers intertwined, on top of the report and looked directly at Virginia.

"Miss Banks. Did you know that Robert owned a gun?" he asked bluntly.

Virginia hesitated just a brief moment then responded with a startled look on her face. "A gun?" she asked in shock. "Why, no, Superintendent Gaster. I had no idea."

Late Afternoon, Tuesday, 24 July 1900, New Orleans

Silas Jackson stood at the upstairs bedroom window looking out while Robert sat on the bed, his back propped up by several pillows and his injured leg outstretched. Martha was down in the kitchen heating up soup for their dinner. Robert still wore his blue pinstripe suit without the jacket. His vest was unbuttoned as was the shirt's collar.

Silas, with his back to Robert, said, "It's a lot worse than you think." He turned to face Robert, "And, I might add, a whole lot worse than you told Martha. I've heard the whole force is out looking for you. Two policemen are dead and one more is in the hospital. Did you do that?"

Robert looked up at Silas and tried to keep his voice calm. "It'll cool down in a couple of days, Silas. I'll be gone the first thing day after tomorrow. My leg's already feeling better."

"You didn't answer my question, Robert," Silas said quietly but with sureness in his voice. "But I think we both know what that answer is."

They remained silent as they looked at each other for a moment. Robert knew Silas and Martha held his future, and possibly his life, in the balance. Silas knew this as well.

"Silas, it was never my intention to create such a serious situation, but I was attacked. I was minding my own business last night when a police officer attacked me, and when I ran away from him he shot at me. I did what was necessary to defend my life. The same with the other two policemen. I could've killed two others, but they were unarmed." Robert made this statement while looking directly at his friend, who just looked back at Robert without saying a word.

Finally, Silas walked to the bedroom door and motioned to Robert. "Martha told you about the closet downstairs? She's set it up for you. Let's get you down there," he said.

Robert slowly got up from the bed and picked up his suit jacket and the Colt pistol lying under it. Robert limped over to Silas, who headed out the door. Robert followed. "I was protecting my life," he said again quietly.

"I know," Silas answered.

Silas descended the stairs first and Robert followed, putting extra weight on the banister as he clutched it with his left hand. They reached a room with no windows. The room was modestly decorated as a sitting room/bedroom, with a fabric-covered folding screen standing behind an armchair with a side table next to it. While the room's main door led to the duplex's entry hall, another inner door remained closed. The ceiling above this door slanted, indicating that part of the room, including this door, was under the stairwell.

Silas walked over to the closed door under the stairs and opened it. Robert looked in to see a small, closet-like room with a low, slanted ceiling. It was dusty and dark, but there was a chair, blanket, bucket, and small furnace in the closet. "Martha put a few things in here so you can hide away for a few days," Silas said. "She'll bring you food and water."

Filled with relief, Robert assured his friend, "Like I said, Silas, I'll be out of here just as soon as possible."

Silas looked directly at Robert and said, "I'm going to bring your rifle and satchel and hide them in here with you. You have to promise to stay put. Use the bucket. Don't come out for anything!"

"I promise to stay put," Robert said.

"You have to promise me one more thing, Robert," Silas said.

"Anything."

"If for some reason they find you in here, tell them you broke in and hid without us knowing about it," Silas said.

Robert nodded vigorously. "Of course."

Robert knew Silas was aware that if he were caught in their house that would be the end for Martha and Silas Jackson. But Robert also knew that Silas would never lie to his wife of over 28 years. With his pledge, Silas could tell Martha truthfully that Robert promised to keep them safe to the best of his ability.

Silas added quickly, "But most important. No shooting inside or outside this house. You go peaceful. I don't want Martha or any of the kids or other people around here to get hurt. You hear me?"

"Loud and clear, my friend," Robert said.

Silas did not doubt, however, that Robert would defend his life against attackers. He didn't blame Robert for that. He just wished that no one else had to die, especially his wife…or Robert himself.

Silas guided Robert into the closet, saying he'd be right back with Robert's things. "Now you go on and get in there, and once you've closed the door, I'll move that folding screen over here in front of it so no one can see there's a door here."

Stooping into the closet, Robert smiled slightly and said, "Okay, Silas, just don't put the screen so close to the door that anyone wonders how I got in the closet after bringing the screen over here."

Silas grinned and slapped Robert on the back. "You are your daddy's boy, Robert," he said. "That brain of yours just never stops working, does it?"

"I can't afford for it to stop," Robert said quietly. "None of us can." Robert paused for a moment then said with all the sincerity in his heart, "Thank you, my friend. And Martha."

Evening, Tuesday, 24 July 1900, New Orleans

As the sun set on New Orleans, rumors about the shooting and Robert's escape had spread throughout the city aided by the afternoon editions of New Orleans' major newspapers, including the *Daily States*. During the day police had rounded up a number of blacks in the vicinity of Robert's room, put them in police wagons, and taken them down to the Sixth Precinct for questioning. Uniformed officers continued to escort blacks roughly either back to their homes or to police stations in different parts of the city. But most blacks had fled to their homes and gone into hiding.

At one point, when Superintendent Gaster had Virginia back in his office to question her, Richards again came into the room with a message for Gaster. The two stepped out of the office for a moment, leaving

Virginia to nervously wonder what more was expected of her. She thought the Superintendent had bought her story about Robert's violence toward her so she wasn't sure what else he wanted. Virginia felt a bit of shame at the thought of betraying Robert untruthfully, but she had no doubt that the man she loved would approve of her tactics to stay as much out of trouble as possible.

At that moment Gaster and Richards, who escorted a fidgeting, anxious black man about Robert's age and height, stepped back into the office. Virginia looked quickly from one man to the other.

"Miss Banks," Gaster asked, pointing to the black man, whose last name happened to be Charles, "is this the Robert Charles you know? Can you positively identify him?"

Virginia knew instantly that this scared man who looked at her with pleading eyes was not Robert. For a split second she thought of identifying this man as the Robert Charles she knew, but the thought slipped away as fast as it had come. Neither could she betray Robert's or her own ethics by declaring this innocent man to be someone he was not, nor could Virginia deny her love for Robert by continuing to lie.

"I have never seen this man before," Virginia told Gaster. "He is certainly not the Robert Charles I know."

Gaster dismissed Richards and the unfortunate Mr. Charles from his office and said to Virginia, "Miss Banks, I think that will be all for today, although you are to stay in your rooms where we can find you in case we have more questions."

Relieved, Virginia stood and looked down at the tired superintendent, "Sir, I will not be going anywhere, and I can assure you that I will answer all questions to the best of my ability." With that statement, she left.[22]

Sergeant Aucoin, looking worn out, was back on the scene at Robert's room, and some people recognized him as one of the policemen at whom Robert had shot. The small clusters of people left in the street were predominantly white men. A few white teenage boys had joined the groups. Only a few women were about, mostly closing up shops along the road. A larger crowd of white men armed with pistols and rifles worked its way down the street.

The man leading the group, Allen Trumble, headed toward a storefront with a couple of small round tables and chairs in front of it. Trumble pulled out one of the chairs and used it to climb on top of a wooden table. He turned his attention to the gathering mass. He shouted, "I say that nigger could be hiding in any one of these houses."

There were shouts of agreement from the crowd, the loudest of which came from armed men who gathered at the front of the mob to cheer on Trumble.

"His colored neighbors may be giving that killer food and shelter right this very minute," Trumble asserted. "Are we going to stand for it?"

The mob answered loudly, emphatically, and in unison, "NO!"

"Of course we're not," Trumble continued. "I say we march through each and every house 'til we find that animal!"

The crowd cheered as the men in the front waved their guns in the air. The police barely managed to maintain control. A man struggled through the crowd and reached Trumble just as he climbed off the table onto a chair. The man stopped Trumble and leaned in to say something into his ear. Trumble climbed back onto the table and waved for the crowd's attention.

Shouting even louder than before, Trumble declared, "Hold it! Hold it! I've just been told that the nigger who done all this killin' has been found and is down at central jail. Let's go get him!"

The mob cheered and rallied until it grew into a frenzy. Even as the crowd's fringes dispersed, the men with guns and a collection of other whites followed Trumble in the direction of the jail with hundreds of more whites joining the mob's ranks as it moved through the streets of New Orleans.

Night, Tuesday, 24 July 1900, New Orleans

Darkness and relative quiet descended over the residential areas of New Orleans, a peace that would not last. Robert, in pain from his wound, folded the blankets Martha had given him into a make-shift bed and stretched out to rest as best he could, especially since he hadn't slept in over thirty-six hours. He remained alert, however, with his Colt poised in his right hand and his Winchester rifle beside him. It was going to be a long night. As the neighborhood in which he was hiding remained relatively quiet, Robert finally drifted to sleep for a few hours.

A crowd of men—some with firearms, others with lanterns—shouted outside the central jail and tried to push through a line of officers who linked elbows and were armed with nightsticks. The mob demanded the release of the prisoner, most of them believing it to be the main culprit, Robert Charles.

"Give us the nigger," the rioting masses shouted.

"A rope and a tree are all the justice he needs," declared others, their fear and hatred so intense and risen to a pitch so fevered that even the love of the God in which they believed did not have the power to break this tumult of violent wrath.

O'Malley returned to Robert's room to collect the rest of the composition books, but, to his dismay, the room had been further ransacked, with most of the furniture destroyed and the books and papers irrevocably damaged. There was no sign of the trunk.

"Damn it all to hell!" O'Malley cursed.

Overnight, Tuesday to Wednesday, 24 to 25 July 1900, New Orleans

The cities' presses ran nonstop, printing thousands of newspapers that editors were determined to have on street corners by daybreak. The most important story in the *Picayune* declared that Robert Charles "...was a desperate black and would be given no chance to take more life."[23]

By Wednesday morning, 25 July 1900, each of New Orleans' newspapers had informed their readers that the mayor of New Orleans was offering a large monetary reward for the capture or death of Robert Charles. This edict was tantamount to the legal sanctioning of mob violence. The notice that ran in the papers stated:

> **$250 REWARD**
> Under the authority vested in me by law, I hereby offer, in the name of the city of New Orleans, $250 reward for the capture and delivery, dead or alive, to the authorities of the city, the body of the Negro murderer,
> **ROBERT CHARLES,**
> who, on Tuesday morning, July 24, shot and killed Police Captain John T. Day and Patrolman Peter J. Lamb, and wounded Patrolman August T. Mora.
> **PAUL CAPDEVIELLE, Mayor**[24]

Chapter 13

Morning, Wednesday, 25 July 1900, New Orleans

With the entire city of New Orleans on alert for a murdering black man intent on killing anyone and everyone—in the minds of New Orleans' government, law enforcement, press, and white citizens—the city was ripe for violence at a level it had never experienced.

It would not be long before mobs of armed whites, unable to unleash their anger, hate, ignorance, and fear on Robert Charles, turned their murderous vengeance on any New Orleans' black citizen who came between themselves and what they perceived to be justice.

They were aided and abetted by a systemic and socially accepted belief that the color of one's skin demanded a different set of rules to law and order, democracy, and human rights. The bottom line, blacks and people of color were inferior to whites in all ways, and, most important, "freed from the restraining influence of slavery, [blacks] were rapidly 'retrogressing' to their natural state of bestiality."[25]

The entrance to the main police station, where Gaster's office resided, was draped in black for mourning. Tired-looking police officers worked at their desks, others dashed about, and most talked among themselves. Sergeant Richards was on the phone at the main desk. He listened intently, nodding his agreement to the person with whom he spoke. He hung up the phone and proceeded to Superintendent Gaster's office.

Gaster, worn out after not sleeping or stopping work in nearly twenty-four hours, sat at his desk writing. His usually perfect appearance showed his fading energy. He looked up at the knock on his door.

"Come," he directed.

Richards entered, stepping forward to Gaster's desk.

"What is it, Richards?" Gaster asked, his voice as tired as his appearance.

"Sir," Richards began. "Reports are coming in about disturbances all over the city, especially down at the central jail and in the suspect's neighborhood. Two Negroes are known to have been killed and several more wounded."

Gaster stood and fastened his uniform jacket's top two buttons. "More white mobs? Not just the one down at the jail?" he asked. "I was told they had that one under control."

"They did…I mean they do, sir," Richards said. "At least part of it. Apparently the rabble-rouser who led the crowd down to the jail has set out with an off-shot group of armed men."

"What the hell?" Gaster exploded. "I ordered every available uniformed man out on the streets, especially down at the jail and in the area where Charles lives."

"Yes, sir. And we did, sir," Richard said. "Practically every man is out on the streets trying his best to keep the peace, even our part-time patrolmen."

"Well, they're obviously not doing their best!" Gaster said, his anger and fear growing.

Gaster paused and took a deep breath to calm his nerves. He knew as well as anyone that his leadership would be critical to regaining and then maintaining control of this city.

"All right, Richards," he stated. "Order each precinct, including this station, to keep only three men on desk and have all the rest dispatched to the areas with the most reports of violence. And make sure they're armed."

Richards scratched down notes while Gaster continued to speak.

"I'll get back in touch with Mayor Capdevielle. I think we're at a point that means calling in state troops. For now, though, don't say a word about that to anyone. You understand me, Richards?"

Richards stopped writing and saluted his superintendent. "Yes, sir," he answered. "If I may, sir," Richards added, "the families of Day and Lamb are asking to see you."

Gaster's shoulders sagged. "We have riots on our hands, Sergeant." He paused. "But we're in this position because Charles ruthlessly slaughtered those brave men. Get with Millie to set up a time for me to see them."

"Yes, sir," Richards said.

"But make sure you let me know, Richards," Gaster stated, "the minute Charles is captured—especially now that the mayor has sent out the call to arms city wide."

"Someone'll get him," Richards responded.

Gaster reached for his phone when Richards left the office.

In the *Daily States* bullpen, reporters worked frantically at their desks—answering and making calls, taking notes, and typing updates. Editor-in-Chief Hearsey sat at his desk reading aloud from a handwritten manuscript to three men sitting across from him, his principal editors, Matthews, Jenkins, and Bates.

Hearsey continued with passion, "'…and this latest incident of total disrespect and hatred for the law clearly shows the rapid reversion of our negro population to a state of total bestiality and immorality. Our wives and daughters have been terrorized long enough by these fiends…these beasts in human form. Are we to stand idly by and watch our civilization crumble at the hands of these monsters?'"

The office was perfectly quiet as Hearsey put the manuscript down and looked up at the other three men. Matthews broke the silence, "Is that the final draft then, Major?"

"Yes, it is," Hearsey confirmed. "Can we still make it to press?"

"We should be able to if I send Marty with it right away," Matthews answered.

"Do it!" Hearsey ordered. Again, his three minions remained silent until Hearsey dismissed them with a wave of his arm and said, "That's it for now."

The other two editors left the office immediately while Matthews took the document Hearsey handed him. He stood a moment as if to say one more thing to his editor, but Hearsey beat him to it. "Now!" he shouted as Matthews scrambled out of the office.

Once in the bullpen, Matthews saw a preteen boy standing at a reporter's desk. Matthews called him over. "Marty, get this to the print shop, pronto!" he demanded, handing the boy Major Hearsey's editorial.

"Yes, Mr. Matthews," Marty said, then hesitated. "Uh…should I wait for this story Smith is working on and those others before going down?"

"No," Matthews answered. "You go on with this one story. I'll send someone else down with the others. And hurry!"

Marty ran out of the bullpen. Matthews turned to have the fullest vantage point of the bullpen. He shouted loudly to get all reporters' attention. "Okay! Listen up!" he called out. "You've each got five minutes to finish up, then hand your stories over to Patty. She'll get them to layout. If the paper's going to be out on the streets by two-thirty, we have to get to press now! So move it!"

Matthews noticed Thomas O'Malley's desk was empty and turned to Billings, who was pulling his story out of a typewriter. "Billings, where's O'Malley?" Matthews asked.

Billings answered while stacking his story pages together and stapling them. "He said something about an interview with the suspect's girlfriend."

O'Malley sat with Virginia in her small sitting room. Her eyes were red from crying. Virginia's roommate, Ernestine, fussed around in the small side kitchen.

Virginia had told O'Malley the same story she told Superintendent Gaster.

O'Malley asked her, "I spent a little bit of time looking around Robert's room, Miss Banks, and I have to tell you, he does not appear to be a violent man. As a matter of fact, Robert Charles seems to be quite educated, and from his journals, he clearly doesn't advocate violence. If anything, he believes in nonviolence. I'm finding it hard to believe that he would assault a woman."

Virginia sat with her hands in her lap and did not look at the reporter. Her shoulders sagged a bit when it became clear to her that this reporter understood Robert as the man she knew, not the man she presented to the police and the press.

O'Malley continued speaking, "I can certainly understand it, Miss Banks, that you must protect yourself, but I am certain that there is a lot more to Robert Charles than is being presented by the police and the newspapers. They're painting him as a brute…a monster motivated only by taking violent revenge on the white race. I do not believe that is who this man really is."

Virginia could not help herself and exclaimed, "Exactly! You've got to make the police see that, Mr. O'Malley! All they were focused on was if Robert had a gun and the shootings. But, please!" Virginia begged. "Don't tell them I said something different."

Thomas leaned toward Virginia. "Did he, Miss Banks? Have a gun?" he asked her quietly.

Virginia looked down at her hands and did not answer at first. When she looked up at the reporter, Virginia asked, "Mr. O'Malley, what do you really want to report? That a crazed Negro with a gun is running around New Orleans killing and wounding police officers? Or that the police and the city of New Orleans may have the wrong impression about Robert Charles? That perhaps his actions were actually reactions to circumstances? I'm getting very mixed messages from you."

Virginia's assertiveness and insight stopped O'Malley in his tracks, but he felt she still did not fully comprehend how dangerous the situation had become. O'Malley urged her, "Miss Banks, the police who searched Robert's room had access to this same information, but their attention is naturally going to be focused on the two dead policemen and, now, all the violence going on in the streets. It would be next to impossible to get them to listen to information about who Robert is as a person if he was the one who shot those officers. Did he have a gun?"

Virginia responded quietly but confidently, "I don't know, and that's all I've got to say." She hesitated a moment before speaking again. "Maybe Robert's friend who was with him could tell you more about what actually happened."

O'Malley shook his head as he stood. "Unfortunately, I can't get to Lenard Pierce. The police have him locked up tight."

Mid-Morning, Wednesday, 25 July 1900, New Orleans

Lenard sat hunched over in his small cell. Ed McCarthy, the merchant seaman arrested for incendiary speech and inciting a riot, was in the pen next to him. Two uniformed policemen, Johnson and Llyod, approached Lenard's cell. McCarthy stepped up to the bars of his cell to hear better what was going on. As Johnson unlocked Lenard's cell door, he said, "You're being moved. Come on."

Deeply frightened and his body overwhelmed by indescribable pain, Lenard remained on the cot. The two policemen entered Lenard's cell, their hands on their batons, ready for trouble. Lenard started shaking and rocking. McCarthy stepped over to the bar closest to Lenard's cell. He couldn't see Lenard, but he knew the young man was in trouble and needed a hand.

"Chin up, Lenard," he said. "It'll be safer for you out of town. These guys will look out for you on the way. Won't you, Officers?"

Patrolman Llyod, smiling down to Lenard, said, "Sure. Now come on, boy. We don't got all day."

Lenard looked up at Lloyd and then to Patrolman Johnson. He didn't see any encouragement in their faces, only judgement.

McCarthy said encouragingly, "The sooner you're away from these mobs, the better, my boy."

Lenard stood hesitantly. He was barely on his feet when Lloyd turned Lenard away from him while Johnson put shackles on Lenard's wrists, pulling them tight behind his back.

McCarthy cringed at Lenard's wail.

Behind the Sixth Precinct at its back-alley entrance, Johnson and Lloyd, with Lenard between them, stepped over to an unmarked covered wagon. The two officers hoisted Lenard into the back of the wagon, which had four policemen already in it. Superintendent Gaster was determined to have Lenard transported safely to Parish Prison.

Even though the wagon was unmarked and had a civilian-dressed driver, the mob in the street could see the wagon coming out of the alley that led to the police station. The mass of rioters, led by Trumble, rushed the wagon, which moved very slowly due to the hundreds of people in the street. Scores of crazed white men and boys pounded on the side of the wagon, shouting, while others threw trash, scraps of wood and cloth, and rotten food at the horses, driver, and police trying to protect the wagon.

Trumble and a score of his followers made it to the wagon's rear. They wrenched the wagon's two half-sized back doors open, only to have the four policemen who stood in front of Lenard aim their rifles directly at the men trying to get at the prisoner, who remained hunched with his back pressed against the front wall of the wagon nearest the driver.

The policemen inside the wagon kept their stance directly in front of their charge, rifles drawn. It was hard to keep their balance as the wagon jerked along, but their orders were to protect Lenard at all costs while transporting him to the Parish Prison outside the city.

Despite the guns aimed at him, Trumble tried to pull himself up in the wagon. The policemen watched as Trumble grabbed hold of the back right-hand door to pull himself up. When Trumble managed to get a handhold and pull himself halfway inside the wagon, the lead officer, Patrolman Joel, took action. He stepped forward and shouted, "Get yourself down right now!"

His words were drowned out by shouts from the crowd, "Hand him over!...We've got a rope with his name on it!...We want justice!"

As Trumble continued to climb into the wagon, Joel screamed, "Jump down now! I mean it! GET DOWN! I don't want to shoot, but I will if I have to."

Trumble didn't respond. On hands and knees, he crawled forward for better balance so he could stand up and rush this young officer and his colleagues to get to his quarry, a terrorized Lenard Pierce. He genuinely believed that these white police officers wouldn't harm one of their brothers, a white man.

With a bit more confidence and authority, Joel shouted, "You fool! You're thinking we won't shoot, but I have my orders...protect this boy at all costs. BACK...OFF...NOW!"

Trumble started to stand up. Joel rammed the muzzle of his rifle directly into Trumble's chest and moved his finger to the trigger. Trumble stopped. The look of determination on Joel's face convinced Trumble to turn around, scrabble to the open wagon doors, and jump out.

Joel took a couple of unsteady steps to the doors as Trumble fell onto the road. He steadied himself before reaching for the swinging back doors of the wagon and pulling them shut. Joel crawled back to Lenard, who was curled in a fetal position. The young policeman knelt in front of Lenard, breathing very deeply. The other three police officers sat down on the benches on either side of the wagon. Both Joel and Lenard remained on the wagon floor shaking. Neither said a word. The wagon had picked up speed and the sound of the crowd seemed more distant.

Late Morning, Wednesday, 25 July 1900, New Orleans

The day had yet to bring comfort to the city's leaders. Mayor of New Orleans Paul Capdevielle sat in his office along with Superintendent Gaster, a few other city officials, and Major Hearsey, a long-time member of the city council.

Exasperated, Gaster implored, "We can no longer handle this situation by ourselves, Your Honor. We were understaffed and overworked before the rioting. My men just can't be expected to keep order, and, I have to tell you, they're none too happy about the thought of shooting at their own kind."

The Mayor tried to calm Gaster down. "Keep your shirt on, Gaster. I've called the governor, and he's sending some troops. In the meantime, I'm issuing a special call for fifteen hundred civilians to act as a special police force. They'll have their own commander."

Gaster threw up his hand and cried, "But, sir!"

"Who'll report to you, Superintendent. Naturally," clarified Mayor Capdevielle.

The mayor turned to face Major Hearsey. "Now, Hearsey," he started.

"Yes, Your Honor?"

"Can I count on the *Daily States* to run my declaration asking for the restoration of order?" the mayor asked the paper's editor-in-chief. "You know I usually support your paper's position, but this is a state of emergency. I just can't, in my right mind, condone editorials like that last one you wrote. It just makes for more unrest."

"You can count on the *States* to do everything in its power to help you restore peace to our fair city," Hearsey stated with dignity. After all, he, the Major, was a respected member of this city's inner circle not to mention belonging to one of Louisiana's oldest families. He would certainly do what was necessary to restore peace. After all, his agenda of ridding the South of its Negro problem couldn't move forward without law and order.

None of these well-respected city fathers seemed to catch the irony, hypocrisy, or result of calling for chaos one day with an advertisement offering a substantial reward for Robert Charles's capture or death with the plea for peace the next.

"Good," the mayor said as his telephone rang. Mayor Capdevielle answered, "Yes, this is he. Yes…uh huh…certainly…thank you, sir." The mayor hung up the phone and turned back to Gaster, Major Hearsey, and the other city officials.

"The governor has ordered all of the state militia units in our parish and those around us to active duty," the mayor said. "Add that to our special forces and we should have this problem licked in twenty-four hours." The mayor turned to his police superintendent. "Gaster, I want you to turn all of your attention and that of your police force to finding Robert Charles. You leave the rioting to us."

"Yes, Your Honor," Gaster replied with uncertainty but full compliance.

The mayor's aide rushed into the room with a telegram and handed it to Mayor Capdevielle, who read the telegram with a slightly puzzled look on his face. The look turned into amusement as he spoke to his office guests.

"Well, if this doesn't beat all I've ever heard of," he chuckled. "This telegram is an offer of assistance from the 'Citizens Improvement League' in the town of Linville. They're offering to send us enough, in their words, armed and able-bodied white men to, and I quote, 'annihilate the Negroes of New Orleans.'"

The other men murmured at this news while the mayor spoke to his aide, “Send off a telegram respectfully declining this offer.”

“Yes, sir.” The aide took the telegram from the mayor and left the room.

Mayor Capdevielle turned his attention back to Gaster and Major Hearsey. “Let’s keep this offer out of the paper for now, Hearsey, and Gaster, the sooner you find Charles, the quicker this town will be back to normal.”

Both men nodded their cooperation.

Afternoon, Wednesday, 25 July 1900, New Orleans

Robert was seated in the closet on a small chair in the closet in front of the furnace. Using the pipes and bullet mold he had brought with him, Robert was making ammunition. His mind was on his plans to make it through the swamplands surrounding New Orleans and beyond. He knew he couldn’t head east back to Mississippi. His best course, Robert figured, was to head west into Texas and follow the shoreline south into Mexico. He would need as much ammunition as he could make to keep him safe from wildlife—and any other obstacles he encountered—on his escape. He looked up when the closet door opened and Martha handed him a plate of food in his dark hideout. He smiled, taking the plate from her.

"Thanks, Martha. Do you know what's going on out there?" he asked.

"What are you doing?" Martha asked Robert.

"I'm just making sure I have enough bullets for when I head out into the swamp. There are lots of wild animals, and I need to make sure I can protect myself. Now, tell me, what's going on?" Robert asked again.

"I won't lie to you, Robert," Martha reported sadly. "It's not good. Word is there's been trouble, lots of it, for the Negroes in this city. No doubt whites are out for Negro blood."

Robert, despairing, could not look up at Martha. "Oh…dear…God," he murmured. "I never meant for any of this." He paused, looked up at Martha, and spoke with a bit more assurance. "I'll be out of here soon, Martha. Tomorrow at the latest. I promise," he stated.

"Where to, Robert?" Martha asked softly with little hope left in her voice. "There's no place left for you to go."

Robert looked up at Martha with a somewhat disbelieving look on his face. There was still the smallest glimmer of hope—perhaps defiance—in his eyes. Robert's mouth briefly took on his look of fury…clenched teeth, a slight sneer of his parted lips, a tight jaw. With the intake of a deep breath, Robert relaxed his face, and looked at Martha with a hint of optimism.

"I'm not through yet, Martha," Robert stated with full confidence. "My plan is to make it out of the country. But you and Silas will be safe, I promise. Like I said, I'll make my way through the swamp after nightfall."

Early Evening, Wednesday, 25 July 1900, New Orleans

By now, as dusk fell on the beleaguered city, word had spread throughout New Orleans about a meeting of whites to be held at Lee Circle, located at the intersection of St. Charles and Howard Avenues. Here, at the city's center, stood a tall monument of Robert E. Lee. A mob of about 700 people, mostly white men and boys but with some white women scattered in the crowd, rallied. A makeshift podium of wooden crates was set up in front of the monument so that Confederate General Lee looked down on the masses as if urging his henchmen to victory.

A lanky middle-aged white man with a grizzled beard and dirt-smeared clothes made his way to the podium. He shouted to be heard over the crowd. "I'm the Mayor of Kenner. We're about 10 miles or so, but what's happenin' here in New Orleans'…" Shouts from the rabble drowned out the mayor's words. He waved his arms, shouted louder, and eventually quieted the mob enough to be heard.

"'I am from Kenner, gentlemen, and I have come down to New Orleans tonight to assist you in teaching the blacks a lesson. I have killed a Negro before, and in revenge of the wrong wrought upon you and yours, I am willing to kill again. The only way that you can teach these niggers a lesson and put them in their place is to go out and lynch a few of them as an object lesson. String up a few of them, and the others will trouble you no more. That is the only thing to do—kill them, string them up, lynch them! I will lead you, if you will but follow. On to the Parish Prison and lynch Pierce!'"[26]

The mob roared its approval. Soon the masses, which grew by the minute and eventually reached 4,000 strong, were making their way to Parish Prison, intent on capturing Lenard Pierce and stringing him up on the nearest tree. After all, it was clear that the prisoner, a criminal partner of the fiend Robert Charles, was guilty of murder, rape, and overall monsterous behavior.

Thomas O'Malley tried to make sense out of what was happening throughout New Orleans, but his experience told him that there was no rationality to the distorted logic used by a mob. Too much in Southern society of late seemed out of control to Thomas. He kept a file on the increasing number of lynchings taking place throughout the South, but when he heard the current mob was after Lenard Pierce, he immediately thought about Sam Hose and his horrifying death at the hands of a white mob. He removed his notes about Hose from the bottom drawer of his desk.

As Thomas reread about the Sam Hose lynching, he tried to imagine it from the mob's point of view in hopes of better understanding the current situation. It had been barely a year since Georgia whites had exacted a "more just" sentence on Samuel 'Tom' Wilkes, alias Sam Hose[27]—at least in the minds of the people determined to right the wrongs brought down on whites by savage Negroes, from their point of view.

Sam—reportedly a friendly, literate, intelligent, and responsible 24-year-old black man—had put aside a formal education in order to take care of his invalid mother and intellectually disabled brother. He worked diligently to meet his family's financial obligations. But on 12 April 1899, Sam allegedly murdered his boss, Alfred Cranford.

As had been his habit over the past several years, Thomas had investigated charges against blacks from two perspectives—the official police report and the local grapevine. He kept separate notes of each to maintain a clear line between fact and fiction. Of late, that line seemed to be blurred, with the so-called facts presented by law enforcement and the declared "truth" spread by faster-than-wildfire gossip. Rereading his notes, it was clear to Thomas that the line had been obliterated in the Hose case.

Apparently, after asking for time off to visit his ailing mother, Sam's boss pulled a gun on him and threatened to kill Sam. Believing his life was in danger, it was reported that Sam threw the ax he was holding and it hit and killed Cranford. Knowing that he wouldn't receive a fair trial, Sam fled. The parallels with Robert Charles were not lost on O'Malley. He continued reviewing Hose's story, looking specifically for newspaper reports of the crime.

Not waiting for any detailed reports from the police, Georgia newspapers were quick to print suppositions and innuendo. Sam's guilt became the inevitable conclusion, especially with the offer of multiple cash rewards, including from the governor of Georgia, for Hose's capture. Again, the resemblance to Robert's situation was apparent to Thomas.

As both police and public looked for Sam Wilkes, aka Sam Hose, rumors abounded. Given the fear white men had for their women's safety, it wasn't long before stories of rape and child assualt had sketched Sam into the image of a beast. Newspapers gave credence to these rumors, reporting that Sam had raped Cranford's wife and attacked their baby. They described Hose as "'a monster in human form' who gleefully raped Mrs. Cranford and their infant child in front of the dying Mr. Cranford."[28]

Police reports of the interviews detectives had with Mrs. Cranford clearly showed the absurdity of the rape and child assault claims. While his wife did attest to the fact that Sam killed her husband, she was clear on the fact that Sam fled the scene immediately and never even came into her home. She adamantly denied Sam raped her or assaulted her child. However, this information didn't make it to the public, thanks in large measure, Thomas realized, to the shoddy police work on the case as a whole and the purposeful unwillingness of newspapers to seek and report the truth.

Since there were witness accounts that Sam had killed his employer, there seemed no need for an unbiased police or journalistic investigation to determine if Sam had acted in self defense or even if it was accidental. Thomas didn't know the circumstances of Robert's alleged crime other than he apparently had killed two policemen and wounded a third. Without knowing the facts, how could anyone sit in final judgement? Thomas knew the answer to that question all too well, and what happened to Samuel Wilkes, aka Sam Hose, spoke to how justice increasingly was meted out in the South.

What struck Thomas was the foregone conclusion the newspapers reported, even *The Times-Democrat* in New Orleans. Before Sam was even captured reports were printed of the white community's intention of burning Sam Hose alive at the stake.[29] Under the headline, *Georgia Mob Determined to Burn a Wretch,* on the front page of *The Times-Democrat*'s 14 April 1900 issue, Thomas read:

> "Hose may not be caught until noon tomorrow, and it is just as probable that his body will be a mass of cinders within the next five hours.…As soon as captured Hose will be brought to the scene of his crime…and burned at the stake."[30]

An article printed on 16 April 1900 in *The Times-Democrat* reiterated the community's intent to seek mob justice, only in this article the writer initially refused to classify the group of whites calling for Hose's murder as a mob. Instead, the paper wrote:

> "There are no mobs chasing Hose. The parties in pursuit are composed of the best people in this section of the State. Lawyers, doctors, merchants, farmers and every class and creed of men have joined together with but one purpose in view—the avenging of the crime. There is no attempt on the part of anyone to conceal their identity or to defend their action. They do not hesitate to say what they want with the negro.... 'We want to make an example of him. Whatever death is most torturous, most horrifying to the brute, shall be meted out to him when he is caught."[31]

A mob, motivated by cash rewards, apprehended Sam at gunpoint in Newman, Georgia, on 23 April 1899. At first there seemed to be a genuine desire to exchange Sam for the reward money, but as the jailer escorted him to his holding cell, a growing crowd of whites—complete with mob mentality—formed. A member of this mob held a gun to the jailer's head, demanding the prisoner be turned over to the mob. A former Georgia governor and a judge begged the crowd to let the authorities handle the situation. Their pleas fell on deaf ears.

The mob that kidnapped Sam headed back toward the scene of the crime, attracting over 1,000 local followers who would eventually witness Sam's torture and murder. Another 1,000 had taken a train from Atlanta to join the mob in Newman, Georgia. In the end, around 2,000 whites—men, women, and children—participated in and witnessed the horrific murder of Sam Hose.

New Orleans rioters had read newspaper reports of that lynching in Georgia the year before. Thomas rummaged through the articles he had kept from that time and read about Sam's death in the 24 April 1900 issue of *The Times-Democrat*. The account was so long and complete that it went from page one of the paper to page two. New Orleans readers knew the exact torture Sam Hose had suffered at the hands of whites. Thomas began to read the account of Sam's death:

> "Instantly a hand grasping a knife shot out and one of the negro's ears dropped into a hand ready to receive it. Hose pleaded piteously for mercy and begged his tormentors to let him die. His cries went unheeded. The second ear went the way of the other. Hardly had he been deprived of his organs of hearing before his fingers, one by one were taken from his hand and passed among the members yelling and now thoroughly maddened crowd. The shrieking wretch was quickly deprived of other portions of his

> anatomy, and the words, 'Come on with the oil,' brought a huge can of kerosene to the foot of the tree where the negro, his body covered with blood from head to foot, was striving and tugging at his chains....a good supply of brush, pieces of fence rail and other firewood had been placed at the negro's feet. This pyre was thoroughly saturated and a match applied. A flame shot upward and spread quickly over the pile of wood. As it licked the negro's legs he shrieked once and began tugging at his chains. As the flames crept higher and the smoke entered his eyes and mouth Hose put the stumps of his hands to the tree back of him, and with a terrific plunge forward of his body severed the upper portion of the chains which bound him to the tree. His body, held to the tree only as far as the thighs, lunged forward, thus escaping the flames which roared and crackled about his feet. One of the men nearest the burning negro quickly ran up, and pushing him back said: 'Get back into the fire there,' and quickly coupled the disjointed links of chain."[32]

Thomas knew from all the accounts he had read that it took Sam Hose thirty minutes to die once his mutilated body was set afire. These New Orleans whites seeking their own justice for the policemen Robert Charles had killed also knew that the newspapers had portrayed the mob as justice seekers. And fear of being brought to justice themselves did not worry the whites in New Orleans seeking to punish the animalistic crimes of blacks. After all, no one taking part in the 1899 Georgia lynch mob hid their identities. Many even gave their names to journalists, and the New Orleans rioters had read that these people who turned the rule of law into the rule of power received praise for their actions, not punishment.[33]

The deeper understanding of what was happening in his city on this day, Wednesday, the twenty-fifth of July in the year of our Lord nineteen hundred did nothing to help Thomas feel better. His distress, anxiety, and fear only grew worse. Especially knowing that Robert Charles read newspapers daily and would know clearly what fate awaited him if caught by the mob.

The mob that had gathered at General Lee's statue arrived at the front of Parish Prison, where New Orleans' last semblance of what passed for law and order held Lenard Pierce. A determined sheriff's barricade of thirty men armed with Winchesters met the mob. Sheriff Remy Klock, parish of Orleans, stood in front of the barricade and shouted down at the mob, which was chanting for their version of justice. Klock took a strong stance and declared, "There's no way you'll get into this prison, and you will not get Pierce."

Surprised by the opposition to their mission, some members of the mob continued to shout out demands for Pierce in the name of justice, but Klock would have none of that.

"There's not going to be any lynchings tonight," he declared, "so just put that idea out of your heads. I'm warning you right now to leave us alone, and my men here with their guns pointin' right at y'all, will back me up!"

"You ain't protectin' nothin' but a no-good-for-nothin' nigger!" one man yelled.

"He's a citizen of Louisiana just like all of y'all," Klock countered, "and he's entitled to our protection." As he finished making this statement, Klock knew in his heart that logic and law held no bearing to this throng set on vengeance.

A sudden surge from the mob threatened Klock and his men. Klock raised his pistol and shot it up into the air. The armed policemen behind him rushed forward and tried to physically push the crowd down the prison's steps. Fearing bloodshed, some members of the mob stepped back, and, slowly, sections of the crowd dispersed. Offshoots of the group headed in various directions, some of which raided second-hand shops and other places of business to arm themselves with knives, hat pins, horse pistols, and anything else that could be put to use as a weapon.

Night, Wednesday, 25 July 1900, New Orleans

A large splinter group from the Parish Prison mob headed to New Orleans' downtown, an area that remained busy well into the evening. Streetcars ran throughout the district, most of them carrying people home after a long day's work. The mob, several thousand strong and growing more frustrated and frenzied for their lack of success at Parish Prison, entered Canal Street just as a streetcar along the Villere line approached, moving slowly. Members of the mob, many shouting, "Stop the car!", managed to jump onboard and seize the trolley car.

Mostly whites with a few blacks, men and women, rode the streetcar, but at the sight of an hysterical white mob, one black passenger tried to jump off the trolley. Cries of "There goes a nigger!" echoed throughout the mob. The black man managed to lose himself in the crowd for a moment, but soon the stark contrast between his skin color and that of mob members made him an easy target.

He ran for his life from the corner of Canal and Villere to Customhouse Street, but his pursuers kept up, many shooting at him with pistols but missing in the dark. When he reached Customhouse Street, the terrified black man ran from the sidewalk to the middle of the street. This desperate move sealed his fate, as it put him near an arc lamp, in full lit view of the mob. Continuing to shoot at him, one rioter found his target and shot the man.

Wounded, the black man started running again, only to be met head on by another branch of the mob. A large, muscular white man leading this second group grabbed hold of the fleeing man with one hand and hit him fiercely in the head with the other. The wounded man sank to the ground, where he was beaten, kicked, and stamped on by the mob. Barely able to move, he managed to crawl toward the street's gutter, only to be met by another vicious attack. A kick to his head sent the man into the gutter, which rushed with water from earlier rains.

"Pull him out!" Don't let him drown!" several rioters cried.

A couple of other men dragged the battered man out of the slimy, mud-thickened water. Once his head was out of the water and he was no longer at risk of drowning, the black man's rescuers made sure he was still alive. Once certain he was, the mob started beating and kicking him again. Back in the darkened part of the street, every few minutes someone in the mob struck a match and held it to their victim's face to see if he was alive or dead. If alive, the inhuman attacks continued. When convinced he was dead, one man in the crowd stuck his gun's muzzle onto the dead man's chest and yelled, "I'll fix the damn Negro!" and fired.[34]

Late Night, Wednesday, 25 July 1900, New Orleans

Another mob entered New Orleans's red-light district. Most houses were shuttered and dark, but from a few open establishments white women leaned out of the windows or stood on front-door steps cheering the mob along. One branch of the mob encountered an older frightened man walking down the street. The mob stopped him.

One member grabbed the man by the collar and said to the mob member next to him, "I can't tell if he's colored or white."

His companion responded, "He's a nigger all right!"

A third rioter looked closely into the terrified man's face and said, "No way! He's one of us. Leave him alone."

Nervous and shaking, their prisoner said, "He's right! I am white. I'm…I'm just like y'all."

The first mob member grabbed the old man under one armpit and declared, "Let's drag him under a light to see better!"

He and the other two rioters hauled the innocent passerby to a streetlamp. A small group followed. The first mobster held back the larger group while the other two looked more closely at their prisoner.

"Well, I guess you're right, Virgil," Number Two said to Number Three. "He looks white to me."

Number Three, Virgil, laughed and said, "Of course, I'm right. Now let the poor sod go."

Number One let the shaking and crying man go while Numbers Two and Three pushed back on the crowd to let the old man pass through. Instead of heading back into the crowd, the frightened man, a Creole by birth, turned and hobbled off quickly in the opposite direction, not looking back. The splinter group returned to the larger mob.

Another crowd of whites, which Mickey from the lumber mill had joined, turned onto the street of black nightclubs in Storyville, near where Ruby lived. The contrast to the weekend night Robert and Ruby had enjoyed together—filled with strains of jazz and laughter of people enjoying time off from work—was stark. With the bars and cabarets closed and the street deserted, this stretch seemed haunted. Not even a breeze stirred up a whisper of life. The deep silence soon grew into a rabble of chaos as the mob filled the street with hate.

Some distance away at the other end of the street, an old black man staggered out of an alleyway unaware of the mob that had invaded the neighborhood. A shot rang out from the mob, and the old man dropped to the street.

Ruby watched this scene from a darkened upstairs window of the house in which she worked. With a cry, Ruby pushed through the other women in the room and rushed down the interior stairwell. She pushed out the front door and ran to the old man shot down in the street.

Mickey, who had fired the shot, stood over the old man's body. Ruby wrenched him away, sobbing, "Get away from him, you bastard! You killed him!"

Mickey, backing away, somewhat frightened, stuttered, “I didn’t…I didn’t know he was an old Negro. I…I didn’t know. I’m…I’m sorry.”

Ruby ignored Mickey, who turned and ran back to the mob. Ruby knelt beside the body and slowly turned the dead man onto his back. She looked down at Hollering John and wailed. She took his lifeless face in her hands, bent over her dearest friend, and sobbed uncontrollably.

Chapter 14

Early morning, Thursday, 26 July 1900, New Orleans

Mob rule surged throughout the early hours on Thursday, keeping businesses closed, workers at home, blacks and their families hidden, and law enforcement officers desperately trying to bring order to a hopelessly chaotic city. White men and boys, cheered on by white women, chased men, women, and children of color through the streets of New Orleans. No pass was given based on age. The raging mobs attacked people of all ages, including the black community's most senior citizens.

Baptiste Philo, a 75-year-old black man, ran smack into a mob while walking along Kerlerec and North Peters Streets around 2:30 a.m. Thursday. He worked in the French Market and was on his way to work when rioters shot him directly in his abdomen. Baptiste somehow managed to find his way to the Third Precinct police station, where officers called an ambulance. He made it alive to Charity Hospital, but he died shortly thereafter.

It even reached a point where hiding in one's home did not protect some blacks. Splinter mobs invaded blacks' homes under the justification of searching for Robert Charles, whereupon they murdered the blacks they did find at home.

The fact of frenzied violence against New Orleans' blacks culminating in the brutal murder of many innocent people was not what stemmed the tide of this barbarous terror. Only when mob rule struck a noticeable blow on the city's economy did the white elites decide that it was time to exert order on the anarchy. The purpose of restoring peace was not to protect or find justice for the city's blacks. It was, however, absolutely necessary to rescue the city's reputation and protect its financial standing.

The *Times-Democrat* reported:

> "When it became known later in the day that State bonds had depreciated from a point to a point and a half on the New York market a new phase of seriousness was manifest to the business community. Thinking men realized that a continuance of unchecked disorder would strike a body blow to the credit of the city and in all probability would complicate the negotiation of the forthcoming improvement bonds. The bare thought that such a disaster might be brought about by a few irresponsible boys, tramps and ruffians, inflamed popular indignation to fever pitch. It was all that was needed to bring to the aid of the authorities the active personal cooperation of the entire better element."[35]

Afternoon, Thursday, 26 July 1900, New Orleans

Robert cautiously looked out of the closet door into the windowless room. He slipped out of the closet and carefully mounted the stairs to see Silas and Martha, who were in their upstairs bedroom. Robert continued to limp slightly. Silas, standing at the window to look out, quickly dropped the curtain closed when Robert entered the room. Robert sat on the edge of the bed. "I'm heading out for Mississippi tonight like I promised," he said.

"But it's still not safe," Martha worried.

Robert looked directly at Martha and spoke as though he wanted his word to be the last on this subject. "And it's not safe for you with me here," he said.

Silas came over to stand beside the bed and looked down at Robert. "There are probably state troops covering the entire county," he said. "It was in the afternoon papers. Every road will be watched."

"I'll find my way through the swamps," Robert responded. He stood and started pacing, careful not to get too close to the window, even though the curtain was drawn. "Besides," he continued, "I'd rather take my chances out there than stay holed away. Not that I don't really appreciate what you're doing for me. It's just..." Robert made a frustrated gesture with his hands.

Silas walked over to Robert and led him back to the bed. He gently nudged Robert until he sat. "We understand, son," Silas said. "And I hope you make it. I'm not saying I'm glad you killed those men, but it's not my place to judge you. And I do believe in self defense. I trust you did what you felt had to be done. As for you leaving, let's compromise. You can stay hidden here through the day tomorrow and head out at dark Friday night. Maybe things will have calmed down by then. The governor has sent the state militia to calm down the crowds. Now come on back downstairs. You need more rest."

Robert willingly followed Silas out of the room, his head slightly down. He knew some of what was happening throughout New Orleans, and he was very aware of his role in the violence against his community. But his survival and that of Silas and Martha remained the motivating factor in Robert's thinking. It was possible that with another twenty-four hours of the authorities not finding him, Robert thought, they might begin to believe that he had escaped the city. His chances of making it through the dark backwaters and out of Louisiana would be better tomorrow.

The mayor had already given orders for a posse of men to help the police maintain order as well as accepted assistance from the governor. But it was only when the city's economic leaders demanded order on that Thursday afternoon that the mayor and his police force put this assistance into full action. While extra forces on the streets brought a semblance of order to some areas, rioting continued throughout many parts of New Orleans all through Thursday night and into the early hours Friday morning.

Early hours, Friday, 27 July 1900, New Orleans

On Friday, just after midnight, a mob attacked the Mabry home, where Hanna Mabry, a black woman, lived with her husband—David Mabry. Their small cottage was along a darkened, swampside portion of Rousseau Street. Both doors and windows were shuttered, and the couple slept in what they believed to be the safety of their home.

As they slept, a mob of whites began ripping off the shutters and shooting volleys of bullets through the windows. Hanna and David, sleeping in the next room over, were awakened by the noise but didn't have a chance to get out of their bed. The mob stormed the cottage, shooting off about twenty rounds according to neighbors. Hanna was shot and killed. Her husband, sharing their bed, was uninjured, miraculously, but when he saw his wife dead beside him, he scrambled around the house barefooted trying to get away. His feet were lacerated by the broken glass all over the floor.

Police eventually escorted David to the Sixth Precinct, where a medic tended to his wounded feet. A search for the people who had killed Hanna was hampered by jeers of "nigger lovers" from uncooperative white neighbors. The police never did capture any of the white attackers.

Chapter 15

Morning, Friday, 27 July 1900, New Orleans

Gaster sat behind his desk at police headquarters and received a report from Richards. "The special police we swore in and the militia have managed to regain some order, sir," Richards stated, "but I have reports that three more Negroes have been killed and fifteen wounded."

Just as Gaster was about to reply to Richards, Patrolman Manning entered the office holding a nervous black man, Fred Clark, by the left arm. "Sir," Manning began, "this man has some information on Robert Charles."

"Excellent!" Gaster said. "Now, Manning, let him go so he can talk to us."

Manning released Clark's arm reluctantly and took a step back. Clark stood in place, looking nervously at his feet.

Trying to keep it on friendly terms, Gaster asked, "What's your name?"

Still not looking directly at Gaster, Clark said, "Fred Clark, sir."

"And do you know Robert Charles?" Gaster continued.

"Not personally, sir," Clark said. "But I seen him around."

"And where's that? And speak up so I can hear you, Clark," Gaster stated, growing a bit impatient.

"Sorry, sir." Clark looked up and spoke a bit louder. "I've seen him on the street where I live, visiting some folks the name of Jackson," Clark reported.

"Does he visit them often?" Gaster asked.

"Yes, sir," Clark replied. "They friends from way back. He and Martha. That's Mrs. Jackson. Silas, that's Mr. Jackson, Martha's husband, says both this Charles guy and Mrs. Jackson come from the same area of Mississippi."

Not wanting the full family history, Gaster prodded Clark, "Have you seen Charles there in the past day or two?"

"No, sir, but I also ain't seen Silas or Martha come outta their house in the last day or so," Clark said hesitantly.

Gaster thought for a moment. A lot of people, especially Negroes, were staying inside during the rioting. It was certainly much safer that way. Clark not having seen the Jacksons in a few days didn't really mean anything. On the other hand, Gaster did have a direct order from the mayor, who was taking his orders from the governor, to put all the police force's energy into finding Robert Charles. No stone can be left unturned, Gaster thought to himself.

To Richards Gaster said, "Get Porteous to investigate." Turning back to a still-nervous Fred Clark, Gaster said, "Okay, Clark. We appreciate your help. We'll check it out. Give Sergeant Richards here the Jackson's address, and then you can go."

Mid-Morning, Friday, 27 July 1900, New Orleans

O'Malley and a number of other reporters were in the press club taking a much-needed break. Most had not slept in over twenty-four hours. A messenger came running into the room, out of breath.

"It looks like the police have a solid lead on where Charles is hidin' out. Over on Saratoga Street," he told the men.

The reporters, except O'Malley, exited the room en masse. O'Malley turned to Taylor, the bartender, and motioned the messenger to join him at the bar. "Get this man a cold drink to wet his whistle, Taylor," O'Malley said.

Taylor set a glass of lemonade in front of the messenger who gulped half the glass down. "Do you have an address on Saratoga?" O'Malley asked.

"Sure do, O'Malley," the messenger said, wiping his lips with the back of his arm, "but if I recall, there's a lot of houses on Saratoga." The messenger picked up the lemonade and started drinking it again while smiling at O'Malley.

O'Malley shook his head while reaching into his right-hand pants' pocket for some coins. "Damn it all," he sniggered. "You guys are going to bury me in a pauper's grave." O'Malley handed the messenger two coins.

"Quit the whinin', O'Malley," the young man said. "I ain't no goop."[36] The young man continued, "I know full well gettin' the story in the bag is a real lollapalooza for you." He put the coins in his pocket. "I wouldn't be a bit surprised if knowin' you scooped them other reporters fires you up to do the hoochie-coochie when you get yourself home at night." He laughed at his own joke.

O'Malley didn't. "Just give me the address," he said impatiently.

Still snickering, the messenger told O'Malley, "It's Silas and Martha Jackson at twelve-oh-eight Saratoga Street."

As soon as O'Malley finished writing down the address, he ran out of the press club. The messenger turned to leave, when Taylor, the bartender, stopped him. "Where you think you're goin', bonehead?" Taylor asked

"Who you callin' a bonehead? Goop!" Taylor said back to him.

Taylor laughed and said, "I'm callin' the man who owes me for his refreshment a bonehead."

"I ain't no bonehead!" the messenger repeated. "'Sides, O'Malley paid for it."

"Then why did you let him leave 'fore puttin' money down on the bar?" Taylor laughed all the way to the cash register as the messenger threw a coin at him and stormed out of the bar.

"Now who's the goop?" Taylor said under his breath.

After more than two days in the dark, cramped closet beneath the Jacksons' stairwell, Robert grew so restless that it was difficult for him to focus his thoughts. He had been thinking about how to make his escape that evening while keeping Martha and Silas protected, and his plan of making his way through uncharted swampland still seemed the best route to freedom.

As he lay on the folded blanket, his injured leg throbbing less, Robert's thoughts jumped to Virginia. The sense of loss, knowing he would never see her again, almost overwhelmed him—his feelings for her were that strong. And that's what surprised him. He had known her for almost three years, but it was in the past week that he saw her more clearly as a woman of strength, character, intelligence, ambition, and beauty. Thoughts of Virginia led Robert to think about his family and his sense of responsibility.

Certainly a man had a responsibility to his family, friends, and community, Robert believed. He always put family first. Rarely did a month go by that Robert didn't mail money home to his parents as well as to Henry, Elizabeth, and their children, Catalina and young Jacob. His New Orleans' family—Alice, Earl, Mariah, and Luke—remained an active part of Robert's life. His friends did as well. He was always willing to help out when he could, knowing he could count on their help when needed. This thought of duty to family and friends began to place a heavy burden on Robert's thoughts.

All of his reflections these past few days were in the context of what he had done—killed two policemen and wounded another in self defense. Had instinct taken over when Mora attacked him? Why didn't he give himself up at his apartment rather than fight back? How had he ended up in a claustrophobic closet in the home of friends he did not want hurt? How would the massive manhunt for him end?

Robert knew the single answer to each of the questions all too well. The torture and murder of Sam Hose had made an indeliable impression on Robert, as had the lynchings he read about on a regular basis in the New Orleans' newspapers. His fate was sealed the moment he first defended his own life against the attack by a white policeman.

Robert was not fully aware that these thoughts had been brewing within him consciously and unconsciously since Mora had first raised his billet to hit Robert for no legitimate reason. As the questions leapfrogged over themselves in his thoughts, more stream of consciousness than deliberate, Robert said quietly out loud to himself, "I have a responsibility to myself."

Robert's logic and reasoning kicked in. Unless he made sure for himself that he was healthy, able-bodied, and motivated, how could he live up to his responsponsibilities to others? He couldn't. It was that simple. Robert now saw the path he'd just taken, as well as the one on which he was about to embark, with clear eyes. That path held no shadows, ruts, or diversions.

At that moment Robert knew that his beliefs, instinct to survive, and anger at the injustices aimed at him were about to climax. Robert Charles was certain he would meet every challenge before him head on, making a statement that he was a man who deserved to live the freedoms his nation declared belonged to him as a citizen of the United States—or so said the Constitution's 14th Amendment, ratified just twenty-two years earlier. Robert Charles, born in the United States to former slaves, was guaranteed "equal protection of the laws," yet, as Robert knew only too well, that protection would be denied him down to his last breath.

Afternoon, Friday, 27 July 1900, New Orleans

Sergeant Porteous and three policemen stepped down from their horse-drawn patrol wagon a block down from the Jackson house on Saratoga Street. A middle-aged man passed them on the sidewalk. Porteous stopped the passerby and asked, "Do you know which house is Martha's?"

The passerby pointed to a nearby house across the street. "Martha lives in that one over there, the green house next to the white one," he told Porteous.

"Thank you, sir," Porteous said before turning to the other policemen. "Come on, men," he directed them.

Porteous and the three policemen crossed the street, went down three houses, and climbed the stairs to the green-colored house. Porteous knocked on the front door.

An elderly black woman, Martha Williams, answered. “Yes, officers? What can I do you for?” she asked politely.

“Mrs. Jackson,” Porteous said with authority but politely. “I’d like to come inside and have a word with you for just a moment.”

Martha smiled at Porteous and said, “Well, gracious me, officer. I’d love to help you out, but you got the wrong Martha. I’m Martha Williams. Martha Jackson lives down the street at twelve-oh-eight. It’s the house with the prettiest garden.”

One of the three policemen accompanying Porteous snickered at his superior’s mistake, but one of the other policemen jabbed him with his elbow to shut him up.

Porteous, who could admit a mistake with the best of them, tipped his hat at Mrs. Williams and said, “Thank you much, ma’am. Sorry to have bothered you.”

Several minutes later the patrol wagon, Porteous, and the three other policemen, pulled up in front of 1208 Saratoga.

Robert, back upstairs for a few moments in the Jackson house, took a quick glance out the window between the curtains. He saw the patrol wagon pull up in front of his friends’ house. Robert dashed as best he could with his leg injury downstairs and hid himself in the closet.

The Jackson house was a smaller dwelling—part of a duplex—to the side of the main house, which had the street numbers 1208 next to the front door. Both residences were two stories, and the Jackson's duplex, and the one where their children lived, was to the left of the main house when facing the two homes. The houses were connected by a small side yard, which had a wisteria-covered path that ran from the side door of the main house to the back side door of the duplex. Both properties were owned by the Joyce's, a white family who lived in the main house and rented out the other dwelling, which Silas and Martha shared with members of their family as well as their renter, Burke.

The small side yard was planted with colorful flowers, and Porteous had to admit it was the prettiest garden on the street, as Mrs. Williams had declared. A second door, closer to Saratoga Street, was along the side of the Jackson house in addition to the farther-back side door. Porteous and one of the three policemen, Corporal Lally, stepped up to the house next to 1208 Saratoga.

Corporal Lally pounded the front door of 1210 Saratoga with his fist and shouted, "Anybody home? Open up, it's the police!"

The dark face of a woman in her late 50s, Imogene Nixon, appeared at the downstairs window to the right of the front door. The window was open slightly and Imogene asked angrily through the crack, "What you want?"

Corporal Lally found his composure and tried to speak more politely. "Can you kindly tell us where

Martha Jackson lives?" he asked. "We were told it was near here at twelve-oh-eight."

Imogene stepped away from the window then appeared at the front door, opening it slightly. "She's next door and across that yard," Imogene said. "Way over there to the right." She pointed across the small garden. Imogene shouted out the front door in the direction of the second house. "Hey, Silas!" she yelled. "There's some policemen out here looking for your wife."

Silas appeared at an upstairs window then disappeared quickly. A few moments later he came out of the first downstairs' side door to his annexed home, the one closest to Saratoga Street. Martha followed her husband outside.

They approached Porteous and Corporal Lally, who had walked past the main house at 1208 Saratoga and started across the small yard toward the couple. Silas and Martha met up with Porteous and Corporal Lally in the middle of the yard.

Remaining natural and cool, Silas asked, "What can I help you with, officers?"

Porteous, affable while authoritative at the same time, said, "We just want to take a look around. Do you mind leading us through this house here connected to the main house? That is where y'all live, isn't it, Mr. Jackson? Mrs. Jackson?"

Martha Jackson began to respond to Porteous, but Silas placed his right arm around her waist and pulled her closer to him. He spoke before his wife could say anything. "This is our home, officer," Silas said, serious but still cordial. "But I can't imagine what you could be looking for. It isn't every day the police stop by and ask to search your home."

"Now, who said anything about doing a search?" Porteous asked, still remaining calm and agreeable.

Martha stepped away from her husband and spoke directly to Porteous. "You did, officer," she said firmly but politely. "You said you wanted to 'take a look around'. Those were the words you used, weren't they? I think that implies a search, which, I believe, gives us a right to know what's going on."

"It's probably nothing at all, ma'am," Porteous tried to reassure her. He paused. "Do you mind if we just step inside with you and your husband?"

Without fear, Martha Jackson said, "Yes, we mind!"

Silas stepped up to his wife and pulled her to him again, speaking quickly to Porteous. "Of course, we don't mind, officer," he said. "I'll take you inside. Martha, would you please go see Imogene and ask if you could use her telephone? Just give Reverend Baldwin a call and see if he can give us a hand."

Martha looked at her husband then walked quickly, almost running, to Imogene's house. Silas turned and walked slowly to the side entrance of his home. Porteous and Lally followed him. Just as he reached the side door, Silas stopped, turned, and looked toward his wife, who was just entering Imogene Nixon's front door. Silas shouted at the top of his voice. "Martha, tell Reverend Baldwin these policemen are wanting to search our house." Silas turned back to face the side door and led the policemen into his home, certain Robert had heard his warning.

Following Silas, Porteous and Corporal Lally stepped into the entry hall that led to the downstairs room, which housed the closet under the stairwell. The room's door was wide open with a view of the entire room.

The folding screen Silas had placed in front of the closet door stood a bit out and to the side of the door. There was a water bucket and dipper atop a little stand beside the chair in front of the screen. Porteous could not see the closet door, which opened a crack. Porteous stepped into the room to take a look around, his interest peaked by the water bucket. He turned to speak to Silas, who stood in the entryway, about six feet from where Porteous stood.

"Hot day like this sure makes a man thirsty," Porteous observed. Porteous turned back to face the screen and walked over to the water bucket, intending to take a drink. From here the policeman could see the slightly open closet door, and he looked directly at it.

Robert thrust his Winchester through the closet-door crack and fired. A bullet pierced Porteous's heart and knocked him backwards. Corporal Lally ran to Porteous. Robert fired again, hitting Lally in the abdomen. Lally fell to the floor, wounded but not dead.

Silas ran frantically out of the room, back down the entryway, and out the side door. "Oh, my God! No!" he shouted. As he dashed through the side yard to Imogene's home, he continued to shout and wave his arms. "Help! Hey! Someone help!"

Silas's shouts attracted the attention of the two police officers who had stayed with the police wagon across the street from the Nixon home. These two officers ran to Silas. His shouts also attracted the attention of Patrolman Peter Fenney, who lived on Saratoga Street and had been awakened by the shooting. He dashed out of his front door two houses down and across the street from the Jackson home. A crowd began to gather in the street, including the reporter, O'Malley.

Robert scrambled out of the closet, bounded over Porteous and Lally, and ran upstairs. He went into the Jackson's bedroom and pressed himself against the side wall that separated this room from the bedroom on the other side of the duplex wall. Using the heel of the shoe on his non-injured leg, Robert began pounding a crawl-through hole between the two bedrooms. He used the butt of his Colt pistol to help make the hole large enough so that he could pass back and forth between the two rooms with relative ease on hands and knees.

After finding out from Silas what had happened, Fenney entered the Jackson home and carefully made his way to the room where Porteous's dead body and the wounded Corporal Lally lay. Lally, who had tried to sit up against the armchair, clutched his stomach-area wound. He looked up desperately at Fenney.

Barely able to speak, he begged, "Fenney. Get me…get me a…a priest, please."

Just as Fenney was going to reassure his dying colleague, Lally warned him, "Careful…he's upstairs…rifle…"

Fenney helped Lally lie back down on the floor and said, “Easy does it, John. Don’t move. I’ll get help.”

“Peter…a priest…hurry,” Lally implored.

Outside the Jackson home the crowd had grown quite large, but it clearly was segregated between whites and people of color, who stayed closer to their homes for easy escape. Most of the whites had made it into the front yard along Saratoga. Several people tried to push their way into the small yard between the Joyce and Jackson homes, but the few police officers on the scene at this point kept them back.

O’Malley and some other reporters on the scene questioned various people who seemed to know what was happening. The two police officers who had accompanied Porteous and Corporal Lally held Silas and Martha Jackson, along with Imogene Nixon, in custody by the police wagon.

Suddenly, Fenney dashed out of the Jacksons’ side door into the small yard and yelled, “Somebody get a priest! Lally’s wounded, and he’s asking for a priest. But be careful. Charles is upstairs and has a rifle. Clear out of the yard!”

No one heeded Fenney’s warning, and people remained cluttered in the front yard within aim of the upstairs windows. Fenney saw a priest pushing his way through the crowd. Father Fitzgerald, who had been attracted to the sight due to the shooting along with the scores of other people gathering in the area, approached Fenney and asked, "Did you say you needed a priest?"

Officer Fenney grabbed Father Fitzgerald by the left arm and hurried him to the side entrance of the Jackson house. "You gotta hurry, Father," Fenney said. "I think Lally's dying. He's gotta have Last Rites."

Both men, with Officer Fenney leading the way, rushed into the Jackson's small home.

Upstairs in the bedroom, Robert sat with his back to the side wall with the crawl-space hole in it. He was to the right of the bedroom's front-facing window. He aimed his Winchester at the bedroom's closed door. He looked back and forth from the door to the window. Although alert and at-the-ready, Robert's demeanor seemed calm and self-assured, even though the noise from the growing mob tried its best to interrupt his careful thoughts.

The outside crowd had grown into a mob with a preponderance of armed white men pushing its way closer to the house. By now, more police officers, deputized citizens, and state militia members had arrived on the scene and were trying to keep the mob in check.

In the downstairs room Father Fitzgerald knelt beside Corporal Lally, who barely held on to consciousness. Father Fitzgerald placed his left hand on

Lally's chest above the bloody wound and made the sign of the cross with his right hand. Officer Fenney stood for just a moment watching the priest perform Last Rites. The noise from the crowd filled the room, making it hard to even hear what the priest was saying. Fenney left the room, running out of the side door and through the small yard toward the crowd, waving both arms at the large mob.

Fenney tried shouting above the crowd's noise, "How 'bout some quiet for the Father! Quiet! For God's sake, give them some peace! It's for Corporal Lally!"

An eerie stillness overcame the part of the crowd closest to the house. As murmurs asking for quiet spread through the horde, a deeper, seemingly reverent—yet curious—silence, shrouded the scene. A 19-year-old white youth, Arthur Brumfield, who had been standing at the front of the crowd nearest the Jackson house, chose that moment to take a step forward with a pistol in his right hand.[37]

Robert moved stealthily to the bedroom's open front window and glanced out of it when the crowd went quiet. Robert saw Arthur Brumfield raising his pistol to the upstairs window as he stepped closer to the Jackson house.

Robert aimed his Winchester at Brumfield and fired, hitting the teenager in the hip. Arthur fell to the ground, wounded. The crowd remained still for a moment, shocked at the sudden rifle shot that had shattered the moment's peace.

Arthur looked up at the window and saw Robert taking aim again. He pleaded out loud, as much to God as to any one person, "Please...dear God...don't shoot!"

Robert Charles fired again from the front upstairs window. Arthur Brumfield dropped dead from a shot through the chest. With the sound of shooting, Father Fitzgerald dashed out the side door. The people in the small side and front yards ran for cover. Thomas O'Malley stepped forward from the crowd and ran to Father Fitzgerald, grabbing hold of his left arm to guide him to safety. O'Malley and Father Fitzgerald made it to the side yard out of view or aim of the upstairs front window.

O'Malley quickly asked Father Fitzgerald, "Is Corporal Lally still alive?"

"Yes, miraculously," the priest said, crossing himself with his right hand.

O'Malley turned to another reporter, Vic Mauberret[42], who had rushed into the side yard next to O'Malley and Father Fitzgerald. "Vic," O'Malley said urgently. "Lally's still alive. We've got to try and get him out of there and to a hospital. Are you willing to give me a hand?"

"Lead the way," Vic said with no hesitation.

Father Fitzgerald said, "I'll take you to him."

The three men, led by the priest, turned to enter the side door. O'Malley stopped before entering and shouted to the men remaining in the front yard. "Can you give us some cover? We're going in after Corporal Lally. Direct your fire into the upstairs windows, not downstairs."

A small crowd of armed white men in the front yard readied their weapons, and when their leader shouted, "Okay, men. Aim high!" guns fired into the upstairs windows.

O'Malley and Mauberret, led by Father Fitzgerald, dashed through the side door, down the entryway, and into the room where Lally lay unconscious.

The shooting continued. A few moments later O'Malley and Mauberret came back out the side entrance carrying Corporal Lally. Mauberret had Lally's feet and stepped out backwards. O'Malley held Lally under his armpits and was followed out the door by Father Fitzgerald, who was praying out loud.

Robert had neither appeared at a window nor made any attempt to fire his Winchester during this fusillade, but a few of the crowd's misfired bullets came dangerously close to the rescuers.

Once the crowd's shooting had started, it could not be stopped. In addition to the armed men in the mob, white men lay on their bellies on various rooftops across the street from the Jackson house with rifles aimed at Robert's fortress. They fired continuous rounds at the upstairs windows. Higher-powered Winchester and Springfield rifles tore through the house's cheap wooden planking, and both the front and side of the Jackson home were riddled with bullet holes.

Robert belly crawled into the other bedroom through the hole in the wall and made his way carefully to the front window. He was just about to pull himself up to look out the window when another round of shooting started. A bullet hit Robert in the shoulder. He fell back on the floor and tried to drag himself under the bed. Another bullet hit Robert, this time in the leg. He was slowed but not incapacitated by his injuries. He pulled himself back to the front window, determined to go down shooting.

Robert appeared every minute or so at one of the front windows, took aim, and fired his Winchester into the crowd outside the Jackson home. Robert held off his attackers for almost an hour and a half, crawling from one bedroom to the next. Each of his carefully aimed rounds, with few exceptions, hit his intended target. Throughout the shooting, Robert killed two white men and wounded nineteen others with his Winchester. He did not use his Colt revolver.

Captain William King of the New Orleans Fire Patrol, along with three additional fire patrol officers, rushed into the side yard between the Nixon and Jackson houses carrying a beat-up twin-sized mattress, a container of kerosene, and a jug of water. Captain King and his men entered the Jackson house through the side door. They hurried into the middle room, where King stopped abruptly at the sight of Porteous's dead body.

He said urgently, yet with frustration, "Damn! We gotta get him out of here." He motioned to the fire patrol officer closest to him. King ordered, "Drag him out to the side yard and get some people to help you carry him to a patrol wagon. We can take it from here."

As one fire patrol officer dragged Porteous's body out of the room, Captain King and the remaining two officers hauled the mattress to the bottom of the stairs. They were accompanied by the sound of Robert and crowd members exchanging gunfire. Captain King poured kerosene on the mattress and set fire to it. He drizzled water expertly on the flames to create thick clouds of smoke. Once the fire and smoke had taken hold, the three men rushed back outside.

Robert moved to the farthest corner of the Jackson's bedroom to distance himself from the smoke coming into the room from under the closed door. Unfortunately, the air was soon thick with smoke, and Robert pulled himself to the bedroom door to open it, letting in greater plumes of thick smoke. He looked out the door down the short hall and saw flames shooting up the stairwell. He rushed across the hall into a smaller closet-like room that Martha used for sewing. He opened the back window and climbed out onto a set of small metal steps leading down to the backyard area of the Jackson house.

Even though most of the mob was at the front of the house, a very-wounded Robert wasted no time hobbling down the stairs and toward the protection of the wisteria-covered path that led from the back side of the Jackson house over to the main house, which the Joyce family had turned over to the police, members of the citizen patrol authorized by the mayor, and a few members of the press.

Five white men—among whom were Thomas O'Malley and a young medical student, Charles Noiret, who had been deputized as part of the citizen patrol—stood in the downstairs side room of the Joyce home, a room facing the Jackson house. The room had a side-door entrance to the small yard just as the Jackson house did. This doorway opened directly on to the wisteria-covered path that connected the two houses.

Under the seeming protection of the vine-covered path, Robert stumbled to the main house with his Winchester at the ready. Just before he reached the side door, it opened and Charles Noiret fired his Winchester rifle at Robert, hitting him in the hip. Robert stopped momentarily and began to give under the weight of the rifle he held and his injuries. He summoned his power, lifted his Winchester, and took a final step through the side door and into the room.

The five men in the side room were startled at Robert's entrance, none more so than Thomas O'Malley, who suddenly realized who Robert Charles was. "Buster," O'Malley called out with alarm.

Robert glanced briefly at Thomas with a look of resignation, but he averted his gaze just as Charles Noiret fired his rifle a second time at Robert, hitting him in the abdomen. O'Malley, frozen with shock, could not stop Noiret or help Robert, who fell on his front just inside the room.

Robert continued to clutch his rifle as he attempted to roll over on his back. Noiret fired three more bullets into Robert's torso. Two other men in the room aimed their weapons and wildly shot into Robert's dead body. Thomas buried his head in his arms and fell back against the wall, sinking to the floor while silent tears spilled down his face.

The outside crowd grew quiet with the sound of all the shooting, but a loud cheer rang out when two of the white men who were inside the side room hauled Robert's bloodied and bullet-ridden body by the feet out the front door.

Silas and Martha Jackon, being held next to the police wagon across the street, looked confused and frightened at all the sudden cheering. As the white men pulled Robert's body across the front yard and onto Saratoga Street toward the police wagon, the Jacksons realized what they were witnessing.

Martha let out a heart-wrenching scream at the site of Robert's brutalized body. Silas tried to wrap his arms around his wife and pull her to his chest to hide the horrific scene from her, but one of the policemen standing guard over the couple grabbed both of Silas's arms and pulled them roughly behind the older black man's back, keeping Silas from comforting his distressed wife. The policeman handcuffed Silas.

Martha reached out to her husband, who she believed was being attacked, and the second policeman grabbed Martha's arms and callously pulled her away from Silas, even as Martha dropped to her knees sobbing.

The cheering crowd watched as Robert's body was dropped on Saratoga Street beside the police wagon. Corporal Trenchard, who had hidden from Robert the first night in Annie Cryder's room and was being accused of lacking bravery, pushed his way through the throng. The crowd urged him on. Trenchard walked up to Robert's dead body and thrust his double-barreled shotgun directly against Robert's bloodied chest. Shouting above the mob's noise, Trenchard yelled, "'Now who says I am a coward?'"[38]

Trenchard fired both barrels, destroying what was left of Robert's chest cavity. The mob rushed forward. While some members of the horde tried to rip away pieces of Robert's clothes as souvenirs, others stomped on his body and head with their boot heels. It took a dozen policemen and another dozen state militia men along with a few citizen police to keep the crowd from stealing and further destroying Robert's body.

Several policemen managed to lift Robert's dripping and mangled body into the back of the police wagon. They put the body in feet first, and dragged it along the wagon's wooden-planked floor between the two rows of open seats inside the wagon. With six armed police officers guarding Robert's body, the wagon moved down Saratoga Street, parting the dispersing crowd. Robert's head, with his face unrecognizable, hung off the back end of the wagon as did his arms, which were stretched out wide, scarecrow-fashion. This inhuman display was the final sight watchers had of this immensely courageous and intelligent man who had fought so hard and with such consideration to protect his humanity.

Lewis Forstall watched from a window, tears running down his face and anger igniting his soul.

Late on a Sunday afternoon, the street where Robert made his last stand was quiet and tranquil. Fred Clark, the informant, sat in a rocking chair on his front porch reading a newspaper. An unidentified black man wearing a dark hood walked down the street toward the Clark house. He mounted the steps to Fred's front porch. Clark rested the newspaper he'd been reading in his lap and looked up at the black man without any great surprise.

"Fred Clark?" the man asked.

"That's me," Fred confirmed.

The black man took a step toward Clark, pulled a revolver out of his right-hand pocket, aimed it at Clark's head, cocked the pistol, and pulled the trigger. There was no shot. Clark, with a startled look on his face, sat frozen. The man cocked the pistol again and pulled the trigger. A bullet ripped through Fred Clark's head.

The black man who killed Fred Clark turned around and removed the hood he wore. Lewis Forstall calmly stepped down the porch stairs, put his revolver in his pocket, and walked away along Saratoga Street.

That same afternoon Virginia Banks cared for the ailing child of her employer. She wore a black armband of mourning, but when asked who had died, all she answered was, “My fiancé.” She received more questions about the small lavender ribbon attached to the armband. To this query she smiled sadly and said, “It is in remembrance for a prince among men.”

Epilogue

The race riots in New Orleans from 24–27 July 1900, resulted in 28 deaths, including the murder of Robert Charles. More than 60 people were wounded in the riots. Blacks made up most of the fatalities and casualties. Twenty-one blacks were killed by the white mobs.

Of the seven people Charles killed, four were police officers—Captain John T. Day, Patrolman Peter J. Lamb, Sergeant Gabriel T. Porteous, and Corporal John F. Lally. Five other officers were dismissed from the New Orleans police force for cowardice, including Corporal Ernest J. Trenchard.

Silas and Martha Jackson, members of their family who lived in the duplex where the standoff took place, Imogene Nixon and her husband, and several other neighborhood blacks were arrested and charged with first-degree murder. The Jacksons went to trial in May 1901, but the judge acquitted them of the murder charges, saying that if they were guilty of anything it was aiding and abetting. No further charges were brought against them. After these acquittals the state dropped its charges against the Nixons and other blacks who had been accused of crimes.

In June 1901, Lenard Pierce, who had been charged with attempted murder of Sergeant Aucoin, was finally released after Patrolman Mora, the first policeman Robert Charles shot, insisted that Pierce never threatened Aucoin or himself.

Of the many thousands of whites—some estimates were of over five thousand—who terrorized New

Orleans blacks during the few days of rioting, only nine white men were charged with murder and none with assault. They were still awaiting trial when the Jacksons, Nixons, Lenard, and the other blacks were acquitted and released. As though it was not acceptable to convict whites of crimes after letting blacks go, all charges were dropped against the nine white men.

The only person who ended up charged, convicted, and sentenced to prison after the rioting and standoff with Robert Charles was Lewis Forstall. He was convicted of manslaughter in 1902 for the death of Fred Clark and sentenced to seven years' hard labor in the Louisiana penitentiary.

Robert Charles's barely recognizable body was identified positively at the city morgue by a number of people who claimed to know him. Among this group was Hyman Levy, the clothing salesman who knew Robert Charles as Curtis Robertson. Levy stated he was surprised that these two men were one and the same. In an interview with a reporter, Mr. Levy was quoted as saying, "'You could imagine my surprise when I [realized] it was Robertson, as I never for an instant thought that he was such a desperate scoundrel.'"[39] Levy also identified the clothes Robert Charles was wearing when he was killed as the blue suit he had recently sold to his customer.

In its Sunday, 26 July 1900 edition, *The Times-Democrat* ran a major headline on page one, "Complete Identification of the Remains of Robert Charles." The article read:

"…Those who were responsible for the disorders of the previous days wisely reached the conclusion that their appeal to *lex talionis* would be met by the majesty of established law, and concluded to curb their passions rather than have them curbed by the constituted authorities.…

"The identification of the remains of the dead desperado was made so complete yesterday as to leave no doubt in the minds of the most skeptical, despite the effort of the mob, with the usual mob intelligence, to batter the murderer's features beyond recognition. In the first place every action of the desperado who was killed in the shack in Saratoga street was in line with that of the man who murdered two police officers and drove four others to cover on Fourth street. There was the same skillful handling of the Winchester, the same abundance of ammunition. His cunning in eluding his enemies, and his success in drawing their fire and its prompt return, showed that the hunted man was the same consistent desperado until the moment when the Winchester ball pierced his vitals.

"But it did not require any such theoretical reasoning to establish the identity of the assassin. There was physical evidence in plenty. The size of the corpse was the size of Charles. The...front teeth were identical, and the clothes of the corpse were the clothes of the murderer. The literature found in the house on Fourth street compared precisely with the literature found in the assassin's room and on his person, and finally those who knew Robert Charles in life had no difficulty in recognizing the remains as his remains. The identification was made by Martha Jackson, who occupied the room from which the murderer "stood off" the besiegers for two hours, and who knew Charles well; by Silas Jackson, who had known Charles a long time; by [Lenard] Pierce, who was Charles' friend and who was with him the night he shot Mora, and by others.

"The identification by Pierce was dramatic and gruesome. The bodies of three negroes were stretched out in the deadhouse. That of Charles was the one farthest removed from the door. The trembling Pierce was told that all that was asked or expected was that he should tell the truth. He was then told to pick out the body of Charles.

> "He looked at the first two bodies quickly, but passed on to the third. There he came to a mass of flesh that was riddled with several ghastly wounds. The face and head had been flattened and mutilated, although the features were all there with the characteristic moustache. Pierce bent over the form, on which the electric light threw a glare that added to the ghastly effect. He appeared puzzled for a moment, and while he was still hesitating one of the men about the morgue, by placing a hand on either side of the battered face, pressed it into something like its natural proportions. As soon as he did so Pierce at once said:
>
> 'That is Robert Charles.'"[40]

That was not Robert Charles. He needs to be known for how he lived his life and the choices he made when his life was threatened—not the inhuman degradation he suffered in death. Robert Charles was buried before dawn on Sunday, 29 July 1900, in an unmarked grave to prevent whites from dismembering his body for souvenirs, which was a common practice at the time. The belief that Robert Charles was an "oddity" and less than human was perhaps best demonstrated when an area sideshow operator offered morgue assistants cash for part of Robert's body prior to burial. Fortunately, this monstrosity did not come about.

However, the people and politicians of New Orleans did their best to erase the memory of this man from the city's history after making sure he was demonized in their present day. They blamed him for the stain of radical racial violence that marred their community's reputation and were much too quick to label him as a violent, white-hating Negro—a 'desperado' as he was described most frequently by all of New Orleans' newspapers. Even moderate newspapers, however, chose to paint him as less than human, as did New Orleans' *The Times-Democrat* issue of 29 July 1900 in the page three article, "Making of a Monster: Something of the Personality of the Arch-Fiend Charles." The article asked:

> ...What matter of a man was this fiend incarnate? What conditions developed him? Who were his preceptors? From what ancestral strain, if any, did he derive his ferocious hatred of whites, his cunning, his brute courage, the apostolic zeal he displayed in spreading the propaganda of African equality? These are questions involving one of the most remarkable psychological problems of modern times.[41]

From the moment I learned about Robert Charles and the New Orleans race riot of 1900, I asked the following questions: What matter of a man was this intelligent, courageous, and diligent person? Who were the people and circumstances of his life that shaped Robert, who believed enough in himself and his worth that he would defend his life to the death? Why did he see migration to Africa as giving him the freedom he knew he deserved as a human being? And it is not so much these questions that involve "one of the most remarkable psychological problems of modern times" but the question of why whites were unwilling or unable to see Robert Charles for his intelligence and experience—not "cunning"; bravery and willingness to do what was right—not "brute courage"; and strong desire to enjoy democracy and all its opportunities—not "zeal [for] the propaganda of African equality"?

Obviously, blacks at that time—and too often today—were not viewed as humans, let alone equals to white. This belief is at the core of white supremacy, which has been a part of American society since this nation's inception. At times people who espouse these radical racist beliefs have been on the fringes of our society. At other times, such as was witnessed on 6 January 2021, this movement has found the spotlight and played a major destructive role in centerline American society and politics. The twentieth century came into being with extreme racism and white supremacy front and center.

Certainly the history and psychology of the white supremacy mindset is complex, but I chose to tell this story to shine a stark light on white inhumane beliefs and behavior put forth by white supremacists as much as to honor a single man's willingness to believe he deserved more in life and work to fulfill that goal. Whites cannot be honest in their own history without both acknowledging the immorality, depravity, and turpitude their race has wrought on blacks and recognizing the humanity, equality, and sacrifice of blacks.

Understanding Robert Charles and the Turn-of-the-Century South

From the later 1880s until about 1915, a Southern white mentality, Radicalism[42]—also referred to as radical racism—penetrated the social, political, economic, and cultural dimensions of white Southern life with disastrous results on the lives of Southern blacks. Radicalism defined black/white race relations of that era, characterized primarily by the nearly complete dehumanization of blacks that necessitated extreme violence in the minds of whites.

This radical way of thinking put forth that slavery had acted as a civilizing influence on black people. Once freed from these constraints, blacks were "retrogressing" to their "natural state of bestiality."[43] Blacks under thirty years old who had been born free, according to this extreme mentality, never experienced the "humanizing improvements" that slavery allowed. This believed retrogressive decay from humanity to bestiality among blacks was the reason so many whites feared the worst possible behaviors on the part of these young black men—assault, murder, and most particularly, rape.

Lynching of black men and boys—and even women— was so prevalent in the late 1800s that the *Chicago Tribune* started keeping records of lynchings in 1882. From 1882 to around 1918, over 3,224 blacks were lynched.[44] According to the *Tribune's* data, over 2,500 black men were murdered by mobs from 1882 through 1899, the numbers per year going from 52 to over 200 each year during 1892 and 1893. By the turn of the century over 100 blacks were being lynched each year. The Equal Justice Initiative's report, Lynching in America: Confronting the Legacy of Racial Terror, "...documents more than 4,400 racial terror lynchings in the United States during the period between Reconstruction and World War II."[45]

Lynching was the overall term given to the killing of blacks at the hands of white mobs. Some blacks were hanged by a rope until dead. Others were beaten, stabbed, kicked, or otherwise assaulted. The worst of lynchings involved burning a human being alive and/or combining this torture with a variety of other assaults as well as using a noose—as in the horrific case of Samuel Wilkes, aka Sam Hose, murdered by a Georgia mob in 1899 as described earlier in this book.

Black men in 1900 had no choice but to fear for their lives when approached by white policemen or citizens intent on accusing them of raping their white women or some other crime against whites. A man as innocent as Robert Charles, sitting on a front stoop waiting on his girlfriend, threatened whites just by being male and having black skin.

When attacked violently, a person will defend himself, herself, or themselves. After all, self preservation is the most powerful human instinct. But the human brain also is driven by the power of thought, as Aristotle so clearly pointed out. "The ultimate value of life depends upon awareness and the power of contemplation rather than upon mere survival," he wrote.

A man of Robert Charles's curiosity, intelligence, and introspection made him a very aware human being—aware of his own self and the society in which he lived. He knew what he wanted from his life and strived through a strong work ethic and the value of relationships to move into a life that would provide him with the freedom, independence, and respect he knew he deserved. Having such awareness—combined with the powerful human instinct to exist against all odds—is possibly what made Robert Charles so adept at defending his life.

Both his brain and body worked in unison as a survival mechanism. Perhaps most important, his determination to learn, expand his horizons, and bridge his American history with his African heritage, gave Robert Charles the adaptability and strength to survive. It was Charles Darwin who said, "It is not the strongest of the species that survive, nor the most intelligent, but the one more responsive to change." But it was centuries earlier that the Namibian proverb stated, "Only the strong survive."

As Professor Hair wrote in *Carnival of Fury*, "Even the hostile New Orleans press of 1900 admitted that few human beings ever fought death as hard as [Robert Charles] did."[46]

Surprisingly, even Major Hearsay in his newspaper, the *Daily States*, admitted he was amazed at Robert Charles's marksmanship and ability to defy capture for three days. The paper and its editor did ultimately blame "northern propaganda" for steeping "his little brain in the poison [of resistance] until his lawless lower centres were raw and inflamed."[47]

The *Daily Picayune* declared that Robert Charles was extremely brave and very determined, but this paper also wrote that he was 'an exception to the rule' compared to other blacks of the time.

Despite his most heinous murder and the attempt of New Orleans' white society to erase his memory, Robert Charles lives on. For a while after his death singers gave voice to *The Ballad of Robert Charles*, before the political danger of championing a militant black man became too dangerous.

Over the next century, many scholars, activists, journalists, and historians of all ranks—both black and white—have remembered Robert Charles out loud so others will understand how important he is in personifying the will of a black person to demand his, her, or their dignity, respect, and right to equal justice. While some have considered him a martyr, Hair, in *Carnival of Fury*, stated that "martyrs seek death, or gladly give up living for the sake of some fixed belief."[48]

Robert Charles wanted to live. He sought and worked toward a life that would provide him with freedom and independence. He died defending his right to live as a fully realized human being, not as a martyr.

This book began with a James Baldwin quote on white supremacy. It ends with his quote on surviving life and letting go of fear and hatred. Robert Charles lived his life and met his death as a survivor who sought redemption through his own self awareness. Hate did not direct his decisions. Self confidence, a sense of self worth, and remarkable courage made him the man he was.

> "That man who is forced each day to snatch his manhood, his identity, out of the fire of human cruelty that rages to destroy it knows, if he survives his effort, and even if he does not survive it, something about himself and human life that no school on earth…can teach. He achieves his own authority, and that is unshakable. This is because, in order to save his life, he is forced to look beneath appearances, to take nothing for granted, to hear the meaning behind the words. If one is continually surviving the worst that life can bring, one eventually ceases to be controlled by a fear of what life can bring; whatever it brings must be borne. And at this level of experience one's bitterness begins to be palatable, and hatred becomes too heavy a sack to carry."
>
> — James Baldwin, *The Fire Next Time*[49]

Author's Note

Robert Charles and the New Orleans Riot of 1900 demonstrated that the beliefs and violent behaviors of whites—lynchings, mob killings, and gruesome torture of blacks—were indicative of a true retrogression of humanity. However, this degeneration was not on the part of blacks, as the white mentality of that time period believed. Rather, the descent into beastiality was by whites who believed in and exerted their perceived superiority. That is the true irony of this historical event. And it is why I believe so strongly that these real people and events need to be shared in a way that brings them back to life.

We must see that the attacks against our nation and its democracy are not by blacks and their supporters who protest over 400 years of enslavement, racism, violence, and discrimination. The retrogression of human decency has come from whites through their attempts to maintain control and protect what they view as their superiority. The hate and fear of blacks by whites was so overwhelming and strong in 1900 that it persists today in 2021, so much so that this nation's former president consciously used the strength of these emotions and beliefs to rally support from current white supremacists, going so far as to incite insurrection, for which he was impeached a second time. It is my observation that for all the progress our nation has made to provide greater opportunities for people from all walks of life—despite persistent and systemic racism—the one mentality that is the least changed is that of white supremacy. As James

Baldwin so astutely noted, "People are trapped in history and history is trapped in them."[50]

In his essay, "Stranger in the Village", which appears in his book *Notes of a Native Son*, Baldwin stated so perfectly this great problem of so many white Americans being unable to let go of their belief in racial superiority. He writes:

> "...confronted with the impossibility of remaining faithful to one's beliefs, and the equal impossibility of becoming free of them, one can be driven to the most inhuman excesses....the establishment of democracy on the American continent was scarcely as radical a break with the past as was the necessity, which Americans faced, of broadening this concept to include black men.
>
> "...But in the situation in which Americans found themselves, these beliefs threatened an idea which, whether or not one likes to think so, is the very warp and woof of the heritage of the West, the idea of white supremacy.
>
> "Americans have made themselves notorious by the shrillness and the brutality with which they have insisted on this idea... The idea of white supremacy rests simply on the fact that white men are the creators of

> civilization...and are therefore civilization's guardians and defenders. Thus it was impossible for Americans to accept the black man as one of themselves, for to do so was to jeopardize their status as white men. But not so to accept him was to deny his human reality, his human weight and complexity, and the strain of denying the overwhelmingly undeniable forced Americans into rationalizations so fantastic that they approached the pathological."[51]

An alarmingly large percentage of America's whites continues to accept the basic tenet that the white race is superior to any other, and too often in recent years, politicians, including our nation's former president, have taken advantage of these peoples' underlying fear of blacks and other people of color to maintain their political, social, and economic power—not just over people of color but also over the very people they look to for support. As James Baldwin so clearly expounds: "White is a metaphor for power...".[52] Without the context of history from a variety of perspectives it is difficult for many whites to see how they are being manipulated.

Shout So Hard to Heaven is an attempt to integrate history with the present. Violence against blacks by whites is an integral part of our nation's history, but the more recent deaths of blacks such as George Floyd and

Breonna Taylor have rallied today's American blacks and their coalition of supporters to rise up and say, "Enough!"

Their historical and modern-day courage and humanity in the face of oppression, violence, and discrimination have inspired and motivated a majority of Americans from many races, ethnicities, and backgrounds.

The centuries of civil disobedience, fights for equal rights, and protests against discrimination is what brought and continues to bring about the changes in our nation toward greater democracy. These movements have been led by blacks, both behind the scenes and in the forefront of the struggle. It is they who have built alliances among people of other backgrounds including whites, indigenous peoples, Hispanics, Asians, and other people of color. The actions and voices—as well as the deaths—of blacks have carried the United States of America to its more perfect union.

The question that has remained for me throughout the writing of *Shout So Hard to Heaven* is, "How can I—a middle-class white woman with the lifelong privileges that come with being born white—adequately tell Robert Charles's story?"

I can never know what it feels like to be black in a nation and society that kidnapped and enslaved my ancestors, spent generations undermining my people's humanity to keep us from participating equally, and defamed the Constitution by murdering and injuring my people—especially black men by police—in an attempt to keep us subjugated. I can try to understand the history and reality, imagining the toll and effects of racism at both its everyday and extreme on individuals. Listening to mothers of black men who have been killed by the police has touched me as a mom. Reading thought-provoking books by black women who trace the importance women of color have had in giving all women more rights has reached me as a female. Appreciating black artists who have used their talents to express their race's struggles has spoken to me as a creative person. But this desire to understand does not mean that I will ever claim, especially with the writing of this book, to be able to speak for blacks about their experiences.

I write and speak as myself, a person passionate about history and storytelling. My professor and mentor, the late Joel Williamson, Ph.D., introduced me to Robert Charles, and suggested I apply my interest in writing to telling Robert's story. My master's thesis was a study of how the portrayal of blacks as "beasts", "animals", and "savages" in Southern newspapers at the turn of the twentieth century contributed to the debasement of blacks by white society. As my research showed, news stories and editorials at the turn of the twentieth century contributed to the normalization of the extreme radical racism that placed whites as superior humans and blacks as subhuman in the mentality of many whites.

This bridge between media communication and the growing mob mentality took place in New Orleans in the years leading up to the 1900 riots, and the white citizens of New Orleans crossed this bridge to the side of anarchy with the portrayal of Robert Charles as a "beast" intent on wreaking havoc and death upon any and all whites he encountered unless he was caught. Unfortunately, these reports fed the flames of radical racism to the point that all New Orleans' blacks were endangered.

The New Orleans race riot of 1900 was neither the first nor the last mob violence whites brought down hard upon blacks at the turn of the century. While each riot had its own circumstance, they shared a core support—a willingness of social, economic, and political leaders to use race to help them further their own agendas of greater power and profit.

The first of these riots was barely two years prior to the violence in New Orleans. In November of 1898, the South "entered yet another phase of heightened violence, a phase that reached its tragic climax in Atlanta in 1906."[53] The 1898 Wilmington riot in my home state of North Carolina has been of particular interest lately as at its core was the deliberate move on the part of a political party, at that time the more conservative Democrats, to use racial division to transcend party lines with the goal of defeating the political joining of the Populist and Republican parties.

As Duke University historian Timothy Tyson clearly showed in his article, "The Ghosts of 1898: Wilmington's Race Riot and the Rise of White Supremacy," North Carolina's Democratic leadership "decided that racist appeals were the hammer they needed to shatter the fragile alliance between poor whites and blacks. They made 'redemption' of North Carolina from 'Negro domination' the theme of the 1898 campaign. Through promising to restore something traditional they would, in fact, create a new social order rooted in white supremacy and commercial domination."[54] Their propaganda centered on words and images that fueled fear of blacks among white citizens, especially poor and undereducated whites, focusing their message on the danger of "black beasts," who the politicians claimed "threatened the flower of Southern womanhood."[55]

My interest in the power of words continues. When I heard first-time presidential candidate Donald Trump declare that Mexican immigrants were rapists, I immediately thought of turn-of-the-century Southern Radicalism and its use of language—especially to encourage fear of rape by men of color—to build white support. In his second run for the presidency, Trump spoke to suburban whites in an attempt to raise their fear about "criminals" (his code for blacks) invading their safe neighborhoods. Trump, throughout both campaigns and his presidency, denigrated people of color by playing on fear-generating stereotypes such as associating them with crime and violence. He misused words with historical significance to blacks and the history of race relations such as comparing his impeachment to a 'lynching'. Perhaps most dangerously, Trump rallied support from white supremacists by refusing to denounce them while openly supporting them with statements such as "stand back and stand by". Trump and Republican messages, just as the 1898 political messages in North Carolina, were designed to speak directly to whites and divide the races in an attempt for "redemption," or in Trump's language, to Make America Great Again.

His final 'grand act' as president of the United States of America was to inspire white supremacists, conspiracy-theory supporters, Neo-Nazis, and misguided Trump supporters to storm the nation's Capitol building, a horrifying culmination to his and others' glorification of hatred we all witnessed on January 6, 2021. Trump and the other speakers knew they were addressing an overwhelmingly white crowd of people who held prejudices—some extreme—against people of color, especially blacks. It was people with the same basic mentality of inequality between the races who murdered innocent blacks throughout the city of New Orleans in reaction to their belief that "white reigns supreme" back in 1900.

How people are portrayed, especially by politicians and in the media, does have an impact on attitudes and behavior. I wanted to add the positive power of human communication—especially through storytelling—to provide a more palpable understanding of the history of race relations as it relates to whites' use of violence to keep blacks from being equal partners in our nation. I decided to write Robert Charles's story because I believe it has important common ground with how racism has been used recently as a tool to maintain power. I wanted to provide a definitive bridge between our nation's past and present in a manner that educates and engages with the hope of reaching a larger audience.

I do believe that it has been, is, and will be blacks who bring about the most important changes in our society as related to the pursuit of equality. Perhaps most important for me, I have grown to understand what is meant by *Black Lives Matter*. I grew up believing that the United States of America will not realize the potential of its Constitution as a true democracy until all human beings, regardless of race, gender identity, sexuality, age, religious belief or lack thereof, economic and educational accomplishments, medical/mental statuses, and any other way in which our society tries to define an individual's identity are given equal opportunities and equal treatment under the law.

I learned from my parents—Willis B. and Bernice Dobson Harvey—to both understand and promote the need to learn history from a variety of perspectives, especially from those people whose voices have been silenced for too long. Because of this belief—that an individual, no matter his/her/their identity has a right to be heard—I didn't understand the anger some of my city's blacks felt a number of years ago when I stood up at a public discussion and said, "all lives matter". I was speaking as a person who believes in the equality of all, and at that time I didn't know it was the same call made by many whites who didn't want to see equality among all people. I was naively trying to express universal equality. I continue to feel shame at making that statement publicly. However, I used the experience as motivation to continue my pursuit of listening to and understanding what people with perspectives different from my own had to say.

I now understand the importance of declaring *Black Lives Matter*. The unequal history of our nation between white privilege and being black makes it necessary to state unequivocally that black people have given their lives and souls to help this nation strive to "become a more perfect union." We will not achieve our potential as a nation and a democracy until we hear with full understanding what these three words—*Black Lives Matter*—mean and represent.

Robert Charles understood that his life mattered. He knew that his life could not be defined as separate and distinct from the history of blacks in the United States and how they were first brought to this land. He also understood that the relationships between whites and blacks throughout that history, especially as defined during the time in which he lived, would affect every aspect of his life. His brutal murder, following his attempt at self defence, helped seal another century of whites maintaining their power by telling blacks, "We have the power to destroy you, and it will be in the most cruel, barbarous, and cold-blooded of ways." Whites manufactured a society-wide and centuries-long fear of blacks among whites, but we made sure black people experienced a very real and horrific fear of whites and the power we extolled through extreme violence and murder.

I wish I could separate myself from whites who have wrought violence and discrimination upon people of color by saying I have not judged and never intend to purposefully judge a person based on the color of his/her/their skin. But just as blacks and other subjugated peoples cannot tell their history without sharing what injustices have been brought to bear against them, neither can whites know and understand their story without acknowledging both the horrendous actions of our ancestors and better knowing the true history of blacks by opening our minds to their words, actions, and points of view.

Learning from others' experiences as well as my own has made me the person I am, and through writing I have the opportunity to share myself with others. Robert Charles had that opportunity taken away from him. Worse, he was dehumanized in print so that the final picture of him presented to his contemporaries was not of a man but of a fiendish desperado. I wish Robert's many journals, which contained his own words, still existed so that Robert could speak for himself. In lieu of his first-hand perspective, I wish to end this book on how some of his friends, neighbors, and acquaintances remembered Robert Charles.

A *Times-Democrat* newspaper reporter who did read some of Charles's journals wrote that they "'showed that he had burnt the midnight oil, and was desirous of improving himself intellectually'".[56] Two elderly black women who lived near Robert Charles—Annie Cryder and Fanny Jackson—told a *Daily Picayune* reporter, "'There was an air of elegance about Charles.'"[57] These two women also thought of Robert as a "'scholar'".[58] People who came in contact with Robert Charles in New Orleans were "uniformly impressed by his intelligence and the ease of expression that suggested an educated man."[59]

In her investigations of both Robert Charles and the New Orleans riots, early 1900s journalist and civil rights activist Ida B. Wells-Barnett wrote to Mr. D.J. Flummer, President of The International Migration Society in Birmingham, Alabama.

This organization's pamphlets—*Prospectus of the Liberian Colonization Society*, *Christian Civilization of Africa*, and *The Negro and Liberia*—were found in Robert's room. He shared the Society's non-violent teachings, along with the non-incendiary words of Reverend Turner as expressed in the *Voice of Missions*, throughout his community.

In her queries, Wells-Barnett asked Flummer for information about Charles. In a letter dated 21 August 1900, Mr. Flummer wrote about Robert to Mrs. Wells-Barnett:

> He always appeared to be mild but earnest in his advocacy of emigration, and never to my knowledge used any method or means that would in the least appear unreasonable, and had always kept within the bounds of law and order in advocating emigration.
>
> The work he performed for this society was all gratuitous, and apparently prompted from his love of humanity, and desires to be instrumental in building up a Negro Nationality in Africa. If he ever violated a law before

the killing of the policemen, I do not
know of it.

Yours, very truly,
D.J. Flummer[60]

As is portrayed in this book, Robert Charles mailed a letter some days before the event on 26 July 1900, when he first defended himself. Wells-Barnett learned from Flummer that the Society in Birmingham had received a letter from Robert two days before the July events. This letter is the only writing by Robert Charles known to have survived.

New Orleans, July 1900

Mr. D.J. Flummer:

Dear Sir—I received your last pamphlets and they are all given out. I want you to send me some more, and I enclose you the stamps. I think I will go over in Greenville, Miss., and give my people some pamphlets over there.

Yours truly,
Robert Charles[61]

This letter was written, signed, and mailed by Robert Charles, and memoranda in the letter's margins indicated that the Society had fulfilled Robert's request for more pamphlets, although Robert was killed before receiving them.

Wells-Barnett also received a letter from a New Orleans resident who had known Robert Charles quite well during the time that Robert lived in that city. As a responsible journalist and knowing the trouble this letter's author could be in if his name was revealed, Wells-Barnett withheld the writer's name.

> New Orleans, Aug. 23, 1900
>
> Mrs. Ida B. Wells-Barnett:
>
> Dear Madam—It affords me great pleasure to inform you as far as I know of Robert Charles. I have been acquainted with him about six years in this city. He never has, as I know, given any trouble to anyone. He was quiet and a peaceful man and was very frank in speaking. He was too much of a hero to die; few [can] be found to equal him....[62]

On Wednesday, 25 July 1900, *The Times-Democrat* printed an article about the murder of officers Day and Lamb on its front page. The article continued on page three, which contained information gained from an interview with Lenard Pierce, who had been arrested that first night when Robert was attacked. Lenard described what he remembered of his friend Robert before they went out on that fateful evening of Monday, 23 July 1900. He said that "...Charles was dressed, ready to go out, and was sitting by a little table writing."[63]

That is how I will always picture Robert Charles, a tall and broad-shouldered man with medium-brown skin dressed nicely in a white shirt with tie, a dark jacket and trousers, and a well-worn brown bowler hat...tugging at one end of his long black moustache while writing his thoughts in a composition notebook.

Janet Harvey Clark
July 2021

Notes

[1] Langston Hughes and Arna Bontemps, editors, "Do You Call That a Preacher: Democratizing Heaven", *Book of Negro Folklore* (New York: Dodd, Mead & Company, 1958) pp. 156-157.

[2] James Baldwin, "Stranger in the Village", *Notes of a Native Son* (Boston: Beacon Press, 2012) p. 174.

[3] William Ivy Hair, *Carnival of Fury: Robert Charles and the New Orleans Race Riot of 1900* (Baton Rouge: Louisiana State University Press, 2010) p. 133.

[4] "Making of a Monster." *The Times-Democrat*, 29 July 1900, p. 3. *Newspapers.com*, www.newspapers.com/image/140248879. Accessed 14 January 2021, by subscription.

[5] Joel Williamson, *The Crucible of Race: Black-White Relations in the American South Since Emancipation* (New York: Oxford University Press, 1984) pp. 201-202.

[6] Performance view for "De Day I Was Sot Free! Sam Lucas' Great Songs". *Johns Hopkins University: Sheridan Libraries, The Lester L. Levy Sheet Music Collection, levysheetmusic.mse.jhu.edu*, https://levysheetmusic.mse.jhu.edu/performance/56897. Accessed November 15, 2020.

[7] "In the Evening by the Moonlight" by James A. Bland (1879). *Lyrics.com*, www.lyrics.com/lyric/3360088/Bing+Crosby/In+the+Evening+by+the+Moonlight. Accessed November 15, 2020.

[8] "A la Roquette" by Aristide Bruant. *Genius.com*, https://genius.com/Aristide-bruant-a-la-roquette-lyrics. Accessed November 15, 2020.

[9] "Story of the Massacre and More Soldiers for Manila." *The Daily Picayune*, 16 July 1900, p. 1. *Newspapers.com*, www.newspapers.com/image/28229217. Accessed January 13, 2021, by subscription.

[10] "Muckrakers." *UShistory.org*, www.ushistory.org/us/42b.asp. Accessed November 15, 2020.

[11] William Ivy Hair, *Carnival of Fury: Robert Charles and the New Orleans Race Riot of 1900* (Baton Rouge: Louisiana State University Press, 2010) p. 8.

[12] Langston Hughes and Arna Bontemps, editors, "God, Man and the Devil: He Heard the Bullet Twice", *Book of Negro Folklore* (New York: Dodd, Mead & Company, 1958) p. 135.

[13] Langston Hughes and Arna Bontemps, editors, "Blues", *Book of Negro Folklore* (New York: Dodd, Mead & Company, 1958) p. 375, 'New Orleans' substituted for 'New York' in the lyrics.

[14] Langston Hughes and Arna Bontemps, editors, *Book of Negro Folklore: Blues* (New York: Dodd, Mead & Company, 1958) p. 395.

[15] Langston Hughes and Arna Bontemps, editors, "Animal Tales: De Knee-High Man", *Book of Negro Folklore* (New York: Dodd, Mead & Company, 1958) pp. 19-20.

[16] "By Use of Keyboards." *The Times-Democrat*, 23 July 1900, p. 1, *Newspapers.com*, www.newspapers.com/image/140248803/. Accessed January 15, 2021, by subscription.

[17] "Compulsory School Education (continued)." *The Times-Democrat*, 23 July 1900, p. 9. *Newspapers.com*, www.newspapers.com/image/140248811. Accessed January 15, 2021, by subscription.

[18-19] "Compulsory School Education." *The Times-Democrat*, 16 July 1900, p. 10. *Newspapers.com*, www.newspapers.com/image/140248714/. Accessed January 15, 2021, by subscription.

[20] "British Now at Pretoria." *The Times-Picayune*, 31 May 1900, p. 1. *Newspapers.com*, www.newspapers.com/image/28307731. Accessed November 15, 2020, by subscription.

[21] William Ivy Hair, *Carnival of Fury: Robert Charles and the New Orleans Race Riot of 1900* (Baton Rouge: Louisiana State University Press, 2010) p. 143.

[22] William Ivy Hair, *Carnival of Fury: Robert Charles and the New Orleans Race Riot of 1900* (Baton Rouge: Louisiana State University Press, 2010) pp. 134-135.

[23-24] "Mob Rule in New Orleans: Robert Charles and His Fight to Death, the Story of His Life, Burning Human Beings Alive, Other Lynching Statistics, 1900" by Ida B. Wells-Barnett. Ebook #14976, *Mob Rule in New Orleans*, 2005. *Project Gutenberg: Gutenberg.org*, www.gutenberg.org/files/14976/14976-h/14976-h.htm. Accessed January 19, 2020.

[25] Joel Williamson, *The Crucible of Race: Black-White Relations in the American South Since Emancipation* (New York: Oxford University Press, 1984) p. 111.

[26] "Mob Anger Vented at Random. The Mob Forms." The Times-Democrat, 26 July 1900, p. 9. *Newspapers.com*, www.newspapers.com/image/140248845. Accessed January 17, 2021, by subscription.

[27] William Ivy Hair, *Carnival of Fury: Robert Charles and the New Orleans Race Riot of 1900* (Baton Rouge: Louisiana State University Press, 2010) W. Fitzhugh Brundage, "Forward", pp. xx-xxiii.

[28-29] "Lynching of Sam Hose." *Wikipedia.com*, https://en.wikipedia.org/wiki/Lynching_of_Sam_Hose. Accessed November 15, 2020.

[30] "Georgia Mob Determined to Burn a Wretch." *The Times-Democrat*, 14 April 1899, p. 1. *Newspapers.com*, www.newspapers.com/image/140797938. Accessed January 17, 2021, by subscription.

[31] "Sam Hose Still at Large." *The Times-Democrat*, 16 April 1899, p. 2. *Newspapers.com*, www.newspapers.com/image/140798142. Accessed January 17, 2021, by subscription.

[32] "Burned at the Stake." *The Times-Democrat*, 24 April 1900, pp. 1-2. *Newspapers.com*, www.newspapers.com/image/140799099 and www.newspapers.com/image/140799106. Accessed January 17, 2021, by subscription.

[33] "Lynching of Sam Hose." *Wikipedia.com*, https://en.wikipedia.org/wiki/Lynching_of_Sam_Hose. Accessed November 15, 2020.

[34-35] "Mob Rule in New Orleans: Robert Charles and His Fight to Death, the Story of His Life, Burning Human Beings Alive, Other Lynching Statistics, 1900" by Ida B. Wells-Barnett. Ebook #14976, *Mob Rule in New Orleans*, 2005. *Project Gutenberg: Gutenberg.org*, www.gutenberg.org/files/14976/14976-h/14976-h.htm. Accessed January 19, 2020.

[36] *Goop* was a term for 'stupid person' in the 1900s.

[37] William Ivy Hair, *Carnival of Fury: Robert Charles and the New Orleans Race Riot of 1900* (Baton Rouge: Louisiana State University Press, 2010) pp. 166-167.

[38-39] William Ivy Hair, *Carnival of Fury: Robert Charles and the New Orleans Race Riot of 1900* (Baton Rouge: Louisiana State University Press, 2010) p. 174.

[40] William Ivy Hair, *Carnival of Fury: Robert Charles and the New Orleans Race Riot of 1900* (Baton Rouge: Louisiana State University Press, 2010) p. 182.

[41] "City Resumes Its Usual Quietude." *The Times-Democrat*, 29 July 1900, p. 1. *Newspapers.com*, www.newspapers.com/image/140248877. Accessed January 15, 2021.

[42] "Making of a Monster." *The Times-Democrat*, 29 July 1900, p. 3. *Newspapers.com*, www.newspapers.com/image/140248879. Accessed January 15, 2021.

[43-44] Joel Williamson, "Part Two: The Rage of Radicalism, 1889-1915", *The Crucible of Race: Black-White Relations in the American South Since Emancipation*, (New York: Oxford University Press, 1984) pp. 109-323.

[45] "Lynching In America: Confronting the Legacy of Racial Terror, Third Edition," Equal Justice Initiative, 2017, https://lynchinginamerica.eji.org/report/. Accessed June 27, 2021.

[46] Perloff, Richard M., "The Press and Lynchings of African Americans." *Journal of Black Studies*, vol. 30, no. 3, 2000, pp. 315–330. *JSTOR*, www.jstor.org/stable/2645940. Accessed January 15, 2021.

[47] William Ivy Hair, *Carnival of Fury: Robert Charles and the New Orleans Race Riot of 1900* (Baton Rouge: Louisiana State University Press, 2010) W. Fitzhugh Brundage, "Forward", p. xxvi.

[48] William Ivy Hair, *Carnival of Fury: Robert Charles and the New Orleans Race Riot of 1900* (Baton Rouge: Louisiana State University Press, 2010) p. 179.

[49] William Ivy Hair, *Carnival of Fury: Robert Charles and the New Orleans Race Riot of 1900* (Baton Rouge: Louisiana State University Press, 2010) p. 2.

[50] James Baldwin, *The Fire Next Time* (New York: Vintage International, 1993) pp. 98-99.

[51] James Baldwin, "Stranger in the Village", *Notes of a Native Son* (Boston: Beacon Press, 2012) p. 167.

[52] James Baldwin, "Stranger in the Village", *Notes of a Native Son* (Boston: Beacon Press, 2012) pp. 174-176.

[53] James Baldwin and Raoul Peck, *I Am Not Your Negro* (New York: Vintage International, 2017) p. 23.

[54] Joel Williamson, "Part Two: The Rage of Radicalism, 1889-1915", *The Crucible of Race: Black-White Relations in the American South Since Emancipation*, (New York: Oxford University Press, 1984) p. 189.

[55-56] "The Ghosts of 1898: Wilmington's Race Riot and the Rise of White Supremacy by Timothy B. Tyson." *Poynter.org*, www.poynter.org/maligned-in-black-white/. Accessed January 16, 2021.

[57-58] William Ivy Hair, *Carnival of Fury: Robert Charles and the New Orleans Race Riot of 1900* (Baton Rouge: Louisiana State University Press, 2010) p. 115.

[59] William Ivy Hair, *Carnival of Fury: Robert Charles and the New Orleans Race Riot of 1900* (Baton Rouge: Louisiana State University Press, 2010) p. 41.

[60-62] "Mob Rule in New Orleans: Robert Charles and His Fight to Death, the Story of His Life, Burning Human Beings Alive, Other Lynching Statistics, 1900" by Ida B. Wells-Barnett. Ebook #14976, *Mob Rule in New Orleans*, 2005. *Project Gutenberg: Gutenberg.org*, www.gutenberg.org/files/14976/14976-h/14976-h.htm. Accessed January 19, 2020.

[63] "Negro Kills Bluecoats and Escapes." *The Times-Picayune*, 25 July 1900, p. 3. *Newspapers.com*, www.newspapers.com/image/28307731/. Accessed November 28, 2020, by subscription.

Acknowledgements

In addition to the inspiration from and historical research of Joel Williamson and William Ivy, I would like to thank my family—parents Willis B. and Bernice D. Harvey, husband and child Ron and Kit Clark, son-in-law Sam Glogovsky, aunt Katherine B. Dobson, and brother and sister-in-law Robert and Lynn Harvey—for their unending support and encouragement. My sincere thanks as well to Lilly Reed, an exceptional teenager in my neighborhood who read my first draft and provided invaluable insights and suggestions. Finally, my gratitude to Lori Kron Naughton for guiding me through the challenges and believing that I would find my identity as a writer.

Most important, I acknowledge the courageous patriots of democracy—Blacks who have challenged the status quo, protested injustice and violence, demanded their rights under the Constitution as full and equal citizens of these United States, and pushed me to acknowledge the deeper, richer history of my nation, no matter how difficult.

About the Author

J.H. Clark grew up in the South, born in Lumberton, NC, and lived in South Carolina, Florida, and Kentucky, before moving back to North Carolina for high school and university. Clark earned a bachelor's degree in Interdisciplinary Studies: Southern History, Literature and Folklore & Scriptwriting at UNC-Chapel Hill and was mentored by one of the most well-known historians and authors on Southern race relations, Dr. Joel Williamson.

After a time in Seattle, WA, Clark received a master's degree in Communications at Cornell University, authoring the thesis, *Racist Ideology in Early Twentieth Century Southern Newspapers*, which included a full-length screenplay about Robert Charles from which this book was written.

As a Director of Marketing & Communications at various universities for nearly thirty years, Clark developed and implemented communication plans that increased diversity in university admissions, especially at law schools; wrote, edited and published award-winning alumni magazines; supported fundraising and development services; and communicated effectively with a variety of targeted audiences including the media.

Clark is now a full-time research historian and freelance writer of narratives and screenplays based on history, human equality, and unsung exemplars.